Shoghi Effendi in Oxford

*Thou shalt behold him endowed with the most perfect appear-
ance, supreme capacity, absolute perfection, consummate power
and unsurpassed might. His face will shine with a radiance that
illumines all the horizons of the world; therefore forget this not
as long as thou dost live inasmuch as ages and centuries will
bear traces of him.*

Upon thee be greetings and praise

'Abdu'l-Bahá Abbás[1]

Shoghi Effendi
in Oxford

and Earlier

by

Riaz Khadem

George Ronald
Oxford

George Ronald, *Publisher*
46 High Street, Kidlington, Oxford OX5 2DN

*A catalogue record for this book is available
from the British Library*

ISBN 0–85398–423–9

Cover picture painted by Bridget Kingdon
Cover designed by Alexander Leith
Typeset by Stonehaven Press, Knoxville, Tennessee
Printed in Great Britain

Dedicated to my father,

Zikrullah Khadem,

whose life's yearning was to attain

the good pleasure of

Shoghi Effendi

Contents

Acknowledgements

I owe a debt of gratitude to Marion Hofman, the tireless and devoted worker in the Cause of God who encouraged me every time we met during the period I was a student at Balliol College. In recent years, her indomitable husband, retired member of the Universal House of Justice David Hofman, has continued the same loving encouragement by instilling a vision of the importance and necessity of this work and has constantly urged me to finish it as soon as possible.

My gratitude is extended to the National Spiritual Assembly of the Bahá'ís of the United Kingdom and especially to Hugh Adamson for giving me access to the Archives of the National Spiritual Assembly. I thank the Balliol Society for providing the names and addresses of Shoghi Effendi's contemporaries and E. V. Quinn, Balliol librarian, for his assistance in the initial research. I thank Golgasht Mossafáí for taking the photographs of buildings in Balliol and Oxford, and Christine Nicholas and Anne Thorne Munro for their assistance in typing letters to two hundred Balliol men. I thank Balliol and St Catherine's Colleges for allowing documents to be photocopied and I am indebted to those men and women who have written their recollections of Shoghi Effendi.

I am grateful to the National Spiritual Assembly of the Bahá'ís of the United States and to its Bahá'í Publishing Trust for permission to quote selections from *Blessings Beyond Measure* by Ali M. Yazdi, published by them in 1988. I am also grateful to the Bahá'í Publishing Trust of the United Kingdom for permission to quote selections from *The Priceless Pearl* by Rúḥíyyih Rabbaní.

ix

I am grateful to Blackwell Publishers for permission to reprint the map of Oxford drawn by Brian Cairns in 1966.

I also thank the members of my family who have encouraged and assisted me with this work, especially my daughter-in-law, Názanín, for helping with the organization of the material, and my wife, Linda, for her careful editing.

Preface

The idea for this book originated one evening in 1965 during a Bahá'í meeting in London when a friend, Mr F. Taghízádih, approached me and asked if I had considered conducting research about the life of Shoghi Effendi at Oxford. I had not, and his question started me on a course that has led to the publication of this book.

The search began one autumn afternoon as I was looking at some old college albums stacked in the Balliol College Junior Common Room. I was curious to see whether Shoghi Effendi's picture might be in one of them. Suddenly my eyes fell upon the face of Shoghi Effendi in the middle of a group of students. I cannot describe the feelings of joy and reverence that overcame me at that moment. With this precious album in hand I hastened to the College office to obtain permission to make a copy of the picture. Permission was granted, and I took the album to Gilman & Soames photo studio. When the photograph was copied, I submitted it to the Universal House of Justice. It now appears in Amatu'l-Bahá's wonderful book, *The Priceless Pearl* and is included here.

The discovery of this precious photograph encouraged me to continue. I approached the Balliol College office to see if they had any records of the student days of Shoghi Effendi. The immediate response was negative. Little was available in the college records after the passage of some 43 years, except a brief description of Shoghi Effendi in the Balliol Registry, and hearsay about the room he occupied in college. Neither did the Local Spiritual Assembly of the Bahá'ís of Oxford have very much detail about the year Shoghi Effendi spent in Oxford. The Balliol College office had been approached before by Bahá'ís. However, the search had not produced significant results and the college offered no encouragement for further research.

I approached Mr Russell Meiggs, Fellow of Balliol and tutor of ancient history, and asked him if he would assist by writing with me the account of Shoghi Effendi's year spent in Oxford. I hoped that Mr Meiggs would help find possible sources of information and would enhance the work with his scholarly approach as an historian. Mr Meiggs graciously accepted my invitation and commenced the joint project by approaching several eminent Balliol men of 1919–21. He was keen to unearth information that would be appropriate for a biography. However, the joint effort did not produce sufficient material and the project was abandoned.

The status of the project was then referred to the Bahá'í World Centre. The response was a letter from the Universal House of Justice stating that 'it was indeed a pity that he [Russell Meiggs] was not able to find sufficient information for you to undertake a biography'.[2]

This letter prompted me to resume the work on my own and to begin a systematic and sustained search. I approached the Balliol librarian, E. V. Quinn, and asked him if he would mind me going through old, dusty archival material in the college library. He consented. This search led me to a few letters about Shoghi Effendi written by his tutor at the Non-Collegiate Delegacy. Upon tracing the history of this institution, it became clear that it had evolved through several stages into St Catherine's College. I then approached St Catherine's College office requesting information about Shoghi Effendi. Most of the important documents presented here were kept in their archives.

Initially, this project was intended to cover only the Oxford period of the life of Shoghi Effendi. I intended to finish the project during my three years of study at Balliol and the subsequent two years I spent at the University of Southampton. However, in the course of the research, I decided to write to the registrar at the American University of Beirut to see if there was any information that would be relevant. By return, the registrar sent some valuable materials including the university transcripts of Shoghi Effendi. As these materials became available about the Guardian's studies in Beirut, I decided to expand the research to include the Beirut years.

An important source, though perhaps less reliable than documents, is the recollection of individuals who had known Shoghi Effendi and could provide anecdotes related to the time they had spent with him. I began looking for professors or other individuals who would have been with Shoghi Effendi at the time but found no one in Oxford. The idea then occurred to me to track down Shoghi Effendi's contemporaries who lived outside Oxford. To do this I needed an address list.

I was pleasantly surprised to find in the college office the names and addresses of 205 men who came to Balliol in the years 1918 through 1921. Those who came in 1918 would have been in their third year when Shoghi Effendi arrived and those who took up residence in 1921 would have had the opportunity of knowing him for three months. I wrote to them all, enclosing a biographical sketch and a copy of a college photograph in which Shoghi Effendi's face was circled.

I was surprised and delighted to receive 135 replies, 52 of which contained some information about or recollection of Shoghi Effendi. I compiled these responses and sent the originals to the World Centre.

Despite diligent search to find the exact room Shoghi Effendi occupied while in Oxford, I was unable to discover any conclusive evidence. There was a rumour attributed to Maurice Keen that Shoghi Effendi occupied the same room he himself had occupied in 1969. Maurice Keen said that he had heard it from his father, Hugh Keen, a Balliol contemporary of Shoghi Effendi. Yet the letter I received from Hugh Keen did not support this view. References Shoghi Effendi had made to pilgrims indicate a general location of the western staircases facing the Martyrs' Memorial.

After much discouragement, I came to feel that perhaps Shoghi Effendi, in his great humility, did not wish his room to be given special significance.

In 1971, having compiled all the available material, I sent the documents to the World Centre for preservation and thus felt that my work was completed, leaving the task of writing the biography to future historians.

Without the continued insistence of two people, my wife, Linda, and Mr David Hofman, I would not have produced this manuscript. I did in fact put it aside for years for two reasons. First, Rúḥíyyih Khánum's book, *The Priceless Pearl*, which is and will always remain the definitive book on Shoghi Effendi, was published, and secondly, I felt that despite all my findings, my search had produced only fragments, tiny pieces of information not sufficient to make a book. I was finally persuaded that all the little bits were priceless too and would be of interest to the believers. During his visit in our home in Peachtree City, Georgia, Mr Hofman reinforced this decision and advised me to commence immediately the task of writing a book based on the original research. In subsequent correspondence and visits with Mr Hofman his advice was amplified.

I started work in 1993 and produced the first draft of the manuscript in 1995. Upon the commencement of this task, I wrote letters to both Balliol and St Catherine's Colleges, where I had found valuable documents 27 years earlier, to see if by chance they had become aware of the importance of documents related to Shoghi Effendi and had collected the material. However, to my disappointment, both colleges

informed me that they had practically nothing of real significance.[3] I was surprised that they did not even list the documents they had given to me some 30 years earlier. Therefore,
I assume the items I had collected are misfiled in the college
archives. Sometime in the future, no doubt, these two colleges
will realize the significance of what they had in their possession and will cherish the legacy of Shoghi Effendi.

Introduction

The transliteration system used in Bahá'í literature is adopted throughout this book except for quotations dating to the period before 1921. These quotations, which are mainly translations of the Tablets of 'Abdu'l-Bahá by Shoghi Effendi or by early believers, are reproduced in their original form. There are a few references to Persian manuscripts which I have translated and these are indicated explicitly in the endnotes.

Significant events in the early life of Shoghi Effendi as a student both in Beirut and Oxford are noted. This book is written in a simple style by an ordinary believer with the assumption that the readers are mainly Bahá'ís. Other readers will find the book of interest once they become familiar with the terminology used in Bahá'í literature.

It is a great privilege for me to write about this subject, a topic that has been dear to my heart all my life. As long as I can remember, the mention of Shoghi Effendi and the attainment of his good pleasure have been the central themes of my life.

During my childhood and youth I learned of Shoghi Effendi through my father's eyes. Later, in 1956 on my own pilgrimage to the presence of the beloved Guardian, a gift I received from my father upon reaching the age of maturity, I had the bounty of confirming through my own experience what I had learned from my father. That pilgrimage allowed me the soul-stirring, priceless and unforgettable experience of standing before the Guardian, gazing at his countenance, walking behind him in the gardens of the shrines, hearing his melodious voice chant the Tablet of Visitation, and pondering his words of counsel and wisdom – words that are still fresh in my memory after the passage of more than 40 years.

Ten years after that pilgrimage, the experience of walking on the same ground Shoghi Effendi's feet had walked, of eating in the same hall where he had taken his meals and studying in the library where he had studied filled my days with feelings that are impossible to describe. I was continually reminded of his presence and the memory of my pilgrimage was vivid throughout my own sojourn in that great academic centre.

To provide a historical context for the reader, I have included a brief history of Balliol College and described some features of that remarkable institution which were unique in 1920 and remain unique today. I have added a few points concerning the attitudes of the British upper class of the time to serve as appropriate social context for the study of Shoghi Effendi's sojourn.

This book contains 18 chapters surveying a period of 24 years in the life of Shoghi Effendi with particular emphasis on his educational experience.

The first chapter, 'Childhood and Youth', is mainly about his elementary and secondary school years. The second chapter, *Syrian Protestant College*, looks at Shoghi Effendi's experience as a student in the preparatory school of this college as well as his undergraduate education. The third through sixth chapters cover a period of about one and a half years after Shoghi Effendi's completion of his studies at the Syrian Protestant College, during which he served the Master as secretary and translator. These chapters provide a brief overview of a few pages from Shoghi Effendi's diary letters recorded by him in Haifa and which he shared with the friends at the time. The seventh chapter, *Recuperation in Paris*, covers a brief period of four months of rest on the outskirts of Paris.

The eighth chapter, *Arrival in England,* looks at the early days of Shoghi Effendi's sojourn in England and at Oxford. Letters written by Shoghi Effendi to several individuals may be found in this chapter.

The next nine chapters are all related to Shoghi Effendi's work at Oxford and are based on records found in Oxford University, letters he wrote, and recollections of his contemporaries. Background information on Balliol College, its layout and social environment is provided.

The last chapter, *The Beloved Guardian,* gives a broad summary of the main points of this book and provides an overview of the period after Shoghi Effendi left Oxford until his passing on 4 November 1957. This chapter conveys my own limited understanding of the unfolding of events during this early period in the Formative Age of the Bahá'í dispensation.

I hope this book will help you draw closer to the beloved Guardian, will assist you in gaining a deeper understanding of the workings of Providence in his life, and will help you appreciate the significance of Shoghi Effendi's contributions to the establishment of the World Order of Bahá'u'lláh.

1

Childhood and Youth

Shoghi Effendi was born on Sunday, 1 March 1897[4] in the house of 'Abdu'lláh Páshá in 'Akká, situated in the vicinity of the barracks where Bahá'u'lláh was imprisoned in 1868. This date of birth is consistent with the information Shoghi Effendi provided on his registration form for the Syrian Protestant College in 1915.[5] Shoghi Effendi's father was Mírzá Hádí Shírází, who was a descendent of the family of the Báb. His mother, Díya'íyyih Khánum, was the eldest daughter of 'Abdu'l-Bahá.[6]

In a Tablet from 'Abdu'l-Bahá we learn of His prayer that God may confer upon His grandson the name Shoghi:

> . . . O God! This is a branch sprung from the tree of Thy mercy. Through Thy grace and bounty enable him to grow and through the showers of Thy generosity cause him to become a verdant, flourishing, and blossoming and fruitful branch. Gladden the eyes of his parents, Thou Who giveth to whomsoever Thou willest, and bestow upon him the name Shoghi so that he may yearn for Thy Kingdom and soar into the realms of the unseen![7]

The title 'Effendi' or Sir, added as a term of respect, is an integral part of Shoghi Effendi's name. The Master required everyone, including Shoghi Effendi's own father, to add the title Effendi to the name and always to address him as Shoghi Effendi.[8]

Shoghi Effendi was one of the 13 grandchildren of 'Abdu'l-Bahá nurtured in the household of the Master. Aware of Shoghi Effendi's great destiny, the Master protected His beloved grandchild by treating him on most occasions the same as the other children. The Master conferred the surname 'Rabbaní', which means 'divine', upon Shoghi Effendi and the younger children of His eldest daughter to distinguish them from the other grandchildren, who used the surnames Afnán and Shahíd.[9]

The earliest records of Shoghi Effendi's schooling are based on the accounts written by Amatu'l-Bahá Rúḥíyyih Khánum. She writes in the *Priceless Pearl* that from childhood Shoghi Effendi had the great desire to write and to learn.

> . . . one day Shoghi Effendi entered the Master's room, took up His pen and tried to write. 'Abdu'l-Bahá drew him to His side, tapped him gently on the shoulder and said, 'Now is not the time to write, now is the time to play, you will write a lot in the future.'[10]

Because of Shoghi Effendi's desire to learn, classes were arranged in the household of the Master for the grandchildren. These classes were taught by an old Persian believer. At one time the children were taught by an Italian, who acted as governess.[11]

When Shoghi Effendi was a young boy the Master sent him with a nurse, Hájar Khátún, to live in Haifa. There he registered in the French Jesuit school, Collège des Frères.[12] Dr Habíb Mo'ayyid, a devoted Persian believer who was in the Holy Land during this period, was assigned by 'Abdu'l-Bahá to look after Shoghi Effendi. Dr Mo'ayyid first met Shoghi Effendi in 'Akká in 1907 and thereafter spent considerable time with him. He states that Shoghi Effendi was not happy in this French school.[13] However, Shoghi Effendi did complete his studies at this school and then went to another Jesuit boarding school in Beirut for advanced studies.

2

Here Shoghi Effendi's unhappiness grew to a point that 'Abdu'l-Bahá arranged for him to transfer to the Preparatory School attached to the Syrian Protestant College of Beirut. A trusted woman was sent by Shoghi Effendi's family to rent a home in Beirut and look after him. But this did not improve the situation.[14]

While attending school in Beirut, Shoghi Effendi spent his vacations in Haifa, often in a small room next to the room occupied by 'Abdu'l-Bahá. He would spend hours studying and reading. At times his lamp remained turned on late at night, and the Master would get up and go to his door, saying 'Enough! Enough! Go to sleep!'[15]

Ali Yazdi was a school friend of Shoghi Effendi, whom he first met in Ramleh, Alexandria, in 1910 when Shoghi Effendi was 13 and Ali Yazdi was 11. Shoghi Effendi had gone to Ramleh to be near 'Abdu'l-Bahá. Here are Ali Yazdi's recollections:

> We slowly started to get acquainted; you know how children are. Then we got to know each other better. I would see him at 'Abdu'l-Bahá's house, and gradually we became friends. Even as a child he was always dignified, but he was also friendly.[16]

Aborted Trip with 'Abdu'l-Bahá

When 'Abdu'l-Bahá returned from His first visit to Europe in 1911, He decided to take Shoghi Effendi with Him to America. At this time Shoghi Effendi was a boy of about 13 years of age. The Master ordered long robes and two turbans for Shoghi Effendi and was pleased to see him try them on.[17] Ali Yazdi recollects Shoghi Effendi's eagerness about this trip to America.

> Shoghi Effendi was in seventh heaven. He had heard so much about America, and he longed to be with the Master

3

as He travelled throughout North America and gave the Message. He looked forward with great anticipation to the experience.

The day before 'Abdu'l-Bahá left, Shoghi Effendi came to see me and asked, 'Sheikh-Ali . . . do you want to go to the ship with me and see my cabin?'

I said, 'Surely!' So, with some other believers, we took the electric train to Alexandria and then to the harbour. Before us was the *Cedric*, a White Star liner.

It was a beautiful ship . . . Shoghi Effendi and I went on the boat, and he took me upstairs and showed me his state-room, the dining room, and everything on the ship. He was extremely happy, and so was I very happy for him. I made him promise to write to me when he got to America, and he said he would.[18]

On 25 March 1912 Shoghi Effendi sailed with 'Abdu'l-Bahá from Alexandria to Naples to commence the long journey to America. However, in Naples the Italian health officials asked him and two other companions of 'Abdu'l-Bahá to leave the ship and return to the Middle East. They said that Shoghi Effendi had trachoma. However, he had never had trouble with his eyes and there were no signs of trachoma. When Shoghi Effendi returned to Ramleh, he consulted doctors who said emphatically that he had no problem whatsoever with his eyes. Yet the damage was done. The young Shoghi Effendi was heartbroken. His separation from the Master was painful. He lost weight and became sick and it took him some time to regain his health.[19]

Dr Mo'ayyid relates that after Shoghi Effendi was denied passage with 'Abdu'l-Bahá to the United States, he went to Beirut:

From Naples Shoghi Effendi proceeded to Beirut to attend school . . . I learned that Shoghi Effendi was not happy with school. He used to pay weekend visits to the Bahá'í students

4

at the Syrian Protestant College (SPC) and stay overnight in my lodgings.[20]

In spirit, Shoghi Effendi was with the Master. He followed the account of 'Abdu'l-Bahá's travels by carefully studying a map of the United States, reading with keen interest every copy of *Star of the West* and tracing His journeys.[21]

'Abdu'l-Bahá's thoughts were also with Shoghi Effendi. He was concerned about Shoghi Effendi's welfare and his happiness. In letters written to the Greatest Holy Leaf, He enquired about His beloved grandson, as these excerpts from different Tablets indicate:

> Write to me at once about Shoghi Effendi's condition, informing me fully and hiding nothing . . .

> Kiss the light of the eyes of the company of spiritual souls, Shoghi Effendi.

> Kiss the fresh flower of the garden of sweetness, Shoghi Effendi.[22]

Furthermore, the Master revealed a Tablet for Shoghi Effendi from America that reflects His love and concern for this precious grandchild:

> Shoghi Effendi, upon him be the glory of the All-Glorious! Oh thou who art young in years and radiant of countenance, I understand you have been ill and obliged to rest; never mind, from time to time rest is essential, otherwise, like unto 'Abdu'l-Bahá from excessive toil you will become weak and powerless and unable to work. Therefore rest a few days, it does not matter. I hope that you will be under the care and protection of the Blessed Beauty.[23]

5

2

Syrian Protestant College (SPC)

When 'Abdu'l-Bahá learned of Shoghi Effendi's unhappiness with the Catholic boarding school in Beirut, He arranged for his transfer to a preparatory school operated by the Syrian Protestant College.[24] Dr Mo'ayyid describes Shoghi Effendi's joy at the prospect of transferring from the French school to the American school:

> I remember Shoghi Effendi took Arabic for his entrance examination into the SPC. He was very happy and always smiled.[25]

A record of Shoghi Effendi's registration at the Preparatory School of this college shows his entrance in October 1912.[26]

Background to the Establishment of the Syrian Protestant College[27]

In the middle of the 19th century, friction between Syrian Muslims and Christians, which had intensified during the period of the separation of Syria from Ottoman rule and its subsequent return to Ottoman control, had reached a crisis point necessitating the intervention of the European powers.

The French government interceded by sending French troops to Lebanon to oversee the situation and to influence the restructuring of the administration of the area. Syria was divided into two provinces, with governors appointed directly by the Sultan, and Lebanon became a separate district with

6

a Christian governor appointed by the Sultan but acceptable to the European powers.[28]

The new political system opened fresh opportunities for the American missionaries in the region to expand their influence. They became aware of the need to increase their numbers and therefore visualized opening a training centre, an American-style college that would combine Christian ideals with modern practices of Western education.

This training centre would not only supply the needed missionaries but would educate knowledgeable leaders for the country. Designated as the Syrian Protestant College, positioned in the city of Beirut, it was established in 1866 and formally opened its doors to 16 students on 3 December of that same year.[29]

A preparatory school was added in 1872 to improve the level of high school graduates who entered the college. By 1902 the enrolment of the college had reached 600, of which half were students in the preparatory school. The college continued to grow into a full university and later became known as the American University of Beirut.[30]

Shoghi Effendi at SPC

Shoghi Effendi attended SPC high school during the period 1912–13. It was a turbulent period in the entire Middle East region. The Italo-Turkish war spread to the area and brought devastation to the shores of Syria. On 24 February 1912 two Italian warships bombarded Beirut and caused large civilian casualties. The Syrian Protestant College, flying the American flag from its buildings, became a place of refuge. Shoghi Effendi was protected in this environment.

During this period Shoghi Effendi completed his high school senior year at the preparatory school and graduated in early summer of 1913. Upon graduation, he hastened to travel to Alexandria to meet his beloved Master, who had returned from His long journey to the West. The period of separation from his beloved was over, and with great longing Shoghi Effendi attained the presence of the Master in Ramleh on 1 August 1913. At this time he was a youth of about 16.[31]

During the next two-and-a-half summer months the young Shoghi Effendi lived again in the household of the Master. He enjoyed the sweet experience of serving Him by taking down letters He dictated, running errands, receiving visitors at the railway station and occasionally accompanying visitors to the famous park and zoo in Alexandria.[32]

In October 1913 the summer vacation was over and Shoghi Effendi returned to Beirut to commence his college education at the Syrian Protestant College. The course of study he chose to pursue was Bachelor of Arts. His aim was to prepare himself for his future services to the Cause. Most of all he wished to please 'Abdu'l-Bahá, who expected Bahá'í students to exemplify a praiseworthy character and to achieve high standards of academic excellence.

During the first semester of his freshman year at SPC, 1913–14, Shoghi Effendi studied English, Arabic, French, History, Geometry and the Bible. During the second semester he continued with the same subjects, except that History was replaced by Biology.[33]

During the second semester of this academic year Shoghi Effendi participated in a declamation contest. This was conducted in four languages: English, Arabic, French and Turkish. Shoghi Effendi was the winner in the French language contest held on 12 May 1914.[34]

Shoghi Effendi was also involved in theatre. On 13 June 1914 the Student's Union of the Syrian Protestant College presented *The Tragedy of Julius Caesar* at the West Hall Auditorium. Shoghi Effendi's name is mentioned in the cast list under 'Senators, citizens, soldiers and attendants'. It is not clear exactly which role he played.[35]

The Bahá'í students attending the Syrian Protestant College expended their utmost to excel in their studies and to devote time to their Bahá'í services. It is clear that Shoghi Effendi played an important role in guiding the services and inspiring the lives of the small group of students. In a letter written from Beirut on 3 May 1914, he wrote:

> Going back to our college activities our Bahá'í meetings, which I have spoken to you about, are reorganized and only today we are sending letters, enclosing glad tidings of the Holy Land, to the Bahá'í Assemblies in various countries.[36]

After completing his freshman year at SPC Shoghi Effendi returned to Haifa for the summer. He corresponded with friends from different lands who had written to share the news of the progress of the Faith in their areas. One of these believers, Siyyid Muṣṭafá Rúmí from Burma, wrote to Shoghi Effendi sharing the glad tidings of the Cause of God. Shoghi Effendi describes the joy that the news brought to the Master:

> . . . a Holy tender smile ran over his radiant Face and his heart overflowed with joy. I then came to know that the Master is in good health for I recollected his sayings which I quote now. 'Whenever and wherever I hear the glad tidings of the Cause my physical health is bettered and ameliorated.' I therefore tell you that the Master is feeling very well and is happy.[37]

The war in Europe began in August 1914 while Shoghi Effendi was spending his summer vacation with the Master and it gradually spread to Turkey. In late October there were rumours that the war would spread in the region and that Syria was unsafe. These rumours caused many students of SPC to drop out and the numbers enrolled at the college fell from 970 to 817. However, the rumours did not affect Shoghi

Effendi's resolve to go back to Beirut to begin his sophomore year.[38]

The immediate result of the declaration of war was the closing of the French and British schools and the enrolment of some 60 former students of the French schools in the Syrian Protestant College. There was fear among the Christian population that the Turkish government, backed by the Germans, was attempting to stimulate a holy war against the Christians in order to attract the Arab world to their side. In early November a *jihád* was proclaimed by the Shaykhu'l-Islám and was confirmed on 11 November by the Sultan. Many Christians at the Syrian Protestant College anticipated a general massacre. However, the *jihád* failed as Husain, King of Hijáz and the Grand Sherif of Mecca, refused to endorse it.[39]

In December 1914 orders came from Damascus that all members of British and French communities were to be deported. This affected many friends of the faculty of the Syrian Protestant College as well as three doctors who had taken refuge on the campus.

Jamál Páshá, Commander of the Fourth Army and supreme Turkish authority in Syria, inspected the college, was impressed by the relief work being done there and allowed the medical doctors to return to Beirut. Soon after, the government was informed that any wounded soldiers sent to the college hospitals would be treated free of charge. The offer was made possible through the Red Cross and Jamál Páshá accepted it, making the Syrian Protestant College a place of relative safety during the war.[40]

Thus, despite the war, Shoghi Effendi studied in a relatively safe environment. During the first semester of his sophomore year, 1914–15, he studied English, Arabic, French, History, Trigonometry, Physics and the Bible. During the second semester he studied English, Arabic, History,

Analytical Geometry, Elementary Mathematical Analysis, Biology and the Bible.[41]

During this latter semester Shoghi Effendi participated again in extra-curricular activities. On 22 May 1915 the college conducted its annual declamation contest in four languages: English, Arabic, French and Turkish. Shoghi Effendi was again the winner of the contest in the French language.[42]

As the war conditions and the blockade of the coast prevented the Bahá'í students at the Syrian Protestant College, most of whom were Persians, from going home, they spent their summer vacations in Haifa. The anteroom to the Shrine of the Báb was assigned to them. This reinforced their continued friendship with Shoghi Effendi, who would also go to Haifa during the summers. These students participated in the activities at the World Centre and frequently attained the presence of the Master.

The Master was pleased with the work of the students of the Syrian Protestant College and He revealed a Tablet in their honour:

Praise be to God that the Bahai students in Beirut are well known for the beauty of their character, the purity of their deeds, and the loftiness of their morality. From whomsoever one enquires about the Bahai students, one will hear unstinted praise. This is through the favours and bounties of the Blessed Beauty, who has assisted you to attain such a high station. For you have lived in a manner conducive to the glorification of the Cause of God. Baha'o'llah is pleased with you; all the people are pleased with you; I am pleased with you, and the friends of God are pleased with you . . . If one asks any person concerning the Bahai students, he will answer: 'In reality they are intelligent, sober, industrious, diligent, displaying good manners and behaviour and concentrating all their attention on their acquirement of knowledge. They do not spend their time in frivolous amusements and distracting recreations.'[43]

11

This Tablet served to define the Master's expectation of Bahá'í students and to encourage the students at the Syrian Protestant College to excel in their studies and to strive to live a life that was pleasing to the Master.

Dr Habib Mo'ayyid, who himself attended the Syrian Protestant College, relates his recollections of the activities of the Bahá'í students there:

> The number of Bahá'í students at SPC, many of whom were sent by the Master, increased to 35 during this period. As teaching the Faith was forbidden in Beirut, Bahá'í activities consisted of meeting other Bahá'ís. The group of students often used to go on picnics with lunches packed by the school consisting of olives, dates, cheese and bread. The group went to the mountains and rivers in the vicinity of Beirut for the day and returned in the evening. Shoghi Effendi associated freely and on the same level with the other Bahá'ís. He was fond of walking, mountain climbing and swimming in the sea, and he played soccer.[44]

Ali Yazdi gives us a further description and paints a vivid picture of Shoghi Effendi's eagerness and joy while attending the Syrian Protestant College:

> At the college Shoghi Effendi was always jolly, optimistic, and hopeful. He had a wonderful personality. All of a sudden he would burst forth with loud laughter. Or sometimes a smile would break on his face. He had a very small mouth; beautiful, expressive eyes; and very regular, handsome features. He was bouncy. He just bounced.
>
> At college we were in the same dormitory. Shoghi Effendi's room was right across the hall from mine . . .
>
> We would converse on many subjects . . . We often talked to each other about the future. His vision was always of the Faith spreading all over the world and of everybody serving the Cause; these were his only ambitions.[45]

12

During the first semester of his junior year, 1915–16, Shoghi Effendi studied English, Arabic, Logic, Economics, Rhetoric, History, Ethics, Zoology and Chemistry. During the second semester he studied English, Rhetoric, Ethics, History, Logic, Economics, Physics and Chemistry.[46]

During the first semester of his senior year, 1916–17, Shoghi Effendi studied English Rhetoric, Arabic Rhetoric, French, History, Economics, Psychology, Engineering, Law and Astronomy. During the second semester he studied French, History, Sociology, Ethics and Law.[47]

The names of the professors and their assistants who taught these courses are listed in the college catalogue of 1915–16. According to this, the president of the Syrian Protestant College was Rev. Howard S. Bliss. Among the professors were: Jebr Mikha'il Dumit, professor of Arabic; Mansur Hanna Jurdak, professor of Mathematics; Julius Arthur Brown, professor of Physics; Rev. Stewart Crawford, professor of Bible and Ethics; Robert Reed, professor of Social Sciences; James Patch, professor of Chemistry; and Alfred Joy, professor of Astronomy.[48]

As stated earlier, Shoghi Effendi's diligent work at the Syrian Protestant College continued throughout a very difficult atmosphere of conflict. The war brought general misery to the whole region and caused a deterioration of economic conditions. Food supplies dwindled rapidly, even at the college. Actual starvation and disease surrounded the Syrian Protestant College and took the lives of more than 300,000 people in Syria.[49]

Shoghi Effendi was protected during the war because he lived in a college that continued to maintain its neutrality. However, this safe haven was always on the verge of disappearing throughout the whole period. Even during the last months before Shoghi Effendi's graduation the college was in danger. The college was informed that diplomatic relations with the United States had been cut off, and consequently, the College would be closed and taken over by the government. A few days later, however, the statement was modified to indicate that the government would not actually take over the College unless Turkey was at war with the United States. To protect the American institution from the fury of the mob, however, policemen were stationed at the gates. The college remained closed but student life continued as usual. On 5 May the college was informed that it could resume its activities on 7 May. Permission to reopen was partially due to the intercession of Jamál Pá<u>sh</u>á.[50]

The reopening of the college enabled Shoghi Effendi to conclude his course of study and to graduate with the degree of Bachelor of Arts on 13 June 1917.[51]

Shoghi Effendi was one of ten students listed among the college graduating class of 1917. His fellow graduates were Fu'ád Amín 'Abdu'l-Málik of Beirut, Fá'iz As'ad of Beirut, 'Abdu'l-Husain Bakir of Haifa, Alexander Chorbajoglou of Constantinople, Murád Ibrahím Dishshi of Beirut, Taufik Yusuf Kashshu of Haifa, Aflátún Mírzá of London, Joseph Salím Rahwán of Cairo and 'Abdu'l-Rahmán Ramieff of Constantinople.[52]

Shoghi Effendi is registered on the college books again on 9 October 1917 as a 'Grad' student. He entered his name on the registers as 'Showqi Hâdi Rabbâni'. Even at this time he was aware of the necessity of accent marks in Persian and Arabic names when transliterated into English. Many years later he introduced the transliteration system now used in Bahá'í literature.

Three months later, on 15 January 1918, Shoghi Effendi wrote to the Master from Beirut. The English translation of this letter is quoted in *The Priceless Pearl*:

> I have resumed my studies, directing and concentrating all my efforts on them and doing my utmost to acquire that which will benefit and prepare me to serve the Cause in the days to come . . . my love and longing for you . . . I have

14

Shoghi Effendi during his early years

Shoghi Effendi as a youth

Shoghi Effendi, seated third from the right, with the Bahá'ís of Ramleh, Alexandria

Shoghi Effendi about the time of 'Abdu'l-Bahá's travels in North America

Shoghi Effendi at the Syrian Protestant College

Number	Name							Date Oct 14
541	Shawki Hadi Rabbani							1916

Name of Student, in vernacular		Name of Father, in vernacular
شوقی ربانی		میرزا هادی شیرازی

Residence of Student	Vernacular	حيفا	English	Haifa

Address of Parent or Guardian (with titles)	Vernacular	حيفا بوزه میرزا هادی شیرازی
	English merchant	Mirza Hadi Shirazi Caïfa

Beirut Guardian	

Age	Religion	Nationality	Previous School	Department	Class	Day or Boarder	Scholarship Aid
19	Baha'i	Persian	S.P.C.	G	IV	Roomer	

Vac 1916 Aug.   Leaving May 14, 1917

Number	Name in Vernacular	طلبه نك اسمی	عدد
455		شوقی ربانی	٤٥٥

Date Oct 9 1917	Name in English	Shawki Hâdi Rabbâni	مكتبه دخولی تاريخی
			اكتوبر ٩ ١٩١٧

Place and date of birth	Residence	محل اقامتی	محل وتاريخ ولادتی
Acre 1899	Haïfa	حيفا ١٨٩٩	عكا

Nationality	Denomination	Date of last vaccination	صوك آشيلانديغی تاريخ	ملتی	ملتی
Persian	Bahai	July 1917	جولای ١٩١٧	بهائی	ايران

Name, Title Occupation and Residence of Father or Guardian	Hâdi Rabbâni Business Haïfa	هادی ربانی تاجم حيفا	پدر ويا وليسك اسم وشهرت وصنعت وملل اقامتی

Beirut Guardian			Previous School
			SPC

Dep't.	Class	Day or Boarder	Scholarship Aid	Remarks
College	Grad.			

Shoghi Effendi's registration form for the Syrian Protestant College

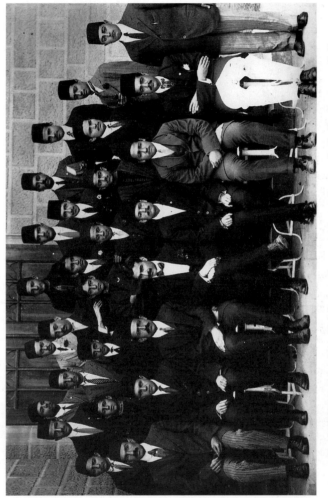

Shoghi Effendi, third from the left, second row, among students at the Syrian Protestant College

Map of the Roman Empire drawn by Shoghi Effendi

sent you by post a piece of cheese, hoping it will be acceptable to Thee.

Thy lowly and humble servant Shoghi[53]

The summer of 1918 was a critical period in the history of the Faith. The Master's life was threatened. Jamál Páshá was determined to crucify 'Abdu'l-Bahá and His family. However, before this appalling act could be carried out, his design was frustrated by the rapidity of the British advance and the entry of General Allenby's forces into Haifa in September of 1918. 'Abdu'l-Bahá was safe.[54]

Though the world war had not yet ended in the summer of 1918, Shoghi Effendi was ready to go back to 'Akká and render whatever service his beloved Master required. He left the American University of Beirut in the summer of 1918 after completing another academic year as a graduate student.

3

In the Service of the Master
Autumn and Winter 1918

The miseries, sufferings and losses experienced by millions during World War I had prepared many receptive souls for the divine message, which the Master had so lovingly delivered on His Western travels. The desire for peace and the prevention of war caused many of these receptive souls to investigate and embrace the Faith. The increase in the number of new believers and the opening of the channels of communication between the Holy Land and the rest of the world brought in hundreds of letters from veteran as well as new believers. Floods of mail poured in from the United States, Germany, France, India, Burma and Persia; letters carrying news of the activities of the believers and their joy at the re-establishment of communications with 'Abdu'l-Bahá. The believers wrote repeatedly to the Master giving Him news of their activities, introducing to Him new believers who had expressed their declaration of faith, asking Him questions about the Cause, seeking His advice on personal decisions and beseeching His blessings, confirmations, guidance and prayers. Such letters were referred to during this period as 'supplications'.

These supplications, many in English, needed to be translated into Persian and the replies of the Master then needed translation into English. The person ideally suited to render this important service was Shoghi Effendi.

16

In addition to the volume of correspondence that flowed into the Holy Land, the removal of restrictions on travel opened opportunities for visitors to journey to the World Centre. The conversations of the Master with the Western visitors also needed translation and Shoghi Effendi was in a position to render this important service as well.

Thus a new chapter opened in the life of Shoghi Effendi, a period of dedicated service to the Master. His service covered a period of about one and a half years, from the summer of 1918 to the spring of 1920. The type of work performed by Shoghi Effendi was uniform throughout this period, consisting mainly of translations for 'Abdu'l-Bahá. However, the volume of the work, as well as the content of the material he translated, varied from month to month. This period of service was perhaps the happiest in his life.[55]

At the beginning of this period, during the winter of 1918–19, Shoghi Effendi translated significant Tablets of the Master in which He showered His love on each one of the believers who wrote to Him. The Tablets show the Master's perfect understanding of the questions the believers had raised as well as questions they had in their hearts but did not mention in their letters. The Master answered them all with the utmost love.

These Tablets were particularly significant because they became the magnets that drew the believers close to 'Abdu'l-Bahá, inspiring many to dedicate their lives to the Faith, striving to reach the station He was calling them to attain. Through such loving correspondence these souls increased their devotion to 'Abdu'l-Bahá and consequently rendered significant services to the Cause of God.

Shoghi Effendi, while serving the Master as a translator, became acquainted with many of these heroes and heroines of the Cause and began correspondence with several of them, correspondence which continued throughout his life. Two

17

such believers were Dr Luṭfu'lláh Ḥakím and Dr John Esslemont. Dr Luṭfu'lláh Ḥakím was from a distinguished Bahá'í family of medical doctors. His grandfather, Ḥakím Masíḥ, the court physician of Muḥammad Sháh, had first caught the spark of faith from Ṭáhirih and was later confirmed in the Cause by one of the Bahá'í prisoners in Ṭihrán. His grandson, Luṭfu'lláh, was born four years before the ascension of Bahá'u'lláh. He grew up in a Bahá'í home. Like his grandfather, he decided to pursue a career in medicine and, when his secondary education was completed, he went to England in 1910 to study physiotherapy. He was an active believer who consecrated his life to the service of the Cause. He attained the presence of the Master many times and wrote to Him frequently.

Dr Esslemont, a medical officer at the Home Sanatorium in Bournemouth, was introduced to the Faith in 1914. His teacher, the wife of one of Dr Esslemont's associates who had met 'Abdu'l-Bahá in London in 1911, recounted her experience while in the presence of the Master and gave Dr Esslemont some pamphlets. The Word of God contained in those pamphlets touched his heart and set him on a course of search that led to his declaration. Just over 12 months after his initial introduction to the Faith, he wrote an inspiring letter to a Bahá'í friend in Manchester that clearly demonstrated the depth of his knowledge and certitude in the Cause of God. While he continued his correspondence with the friends and shared his love for the Cause, Dr Esslemont felt an inner urge to write pamphlets and a book about the new revelation.[56] This intention was communicated to Dr Ḥakím.

When Dr Ḥakím attained the presence of 'Abdu'l-Bahá in Haifa and saw the Master saddened by publications in Europe attacking the Faith, he gave the news of a new believer in the Faith, Dr Esslemont, who had embraced the Cause of God with great enthusiasm. He told the Master that Dr Esslemont

18

desired to write a book about the Faith to 'help the ready souls to reach the fountainhead of love and faith'.[57]

This news pleased the Master. Further mention of the untiring services of John Esslemont, the young doctor in Bournemouth, England, made the Master exceedingly happy. When Shoghi Effendi witnessed the joy in 'Abdu'l-Bahá's countenance, he was prompted to write to Dr Esslemont to convey the Master's pleasure and to deliver the glad tidings that the Master has 'prayed for you and asked His Heavenly Father for confirmation and help'. Shoghi Effendi continued:

> I now hasten, altho late at night, to open a correspondence with you which shall be continuous, inspiring, and regular.[58]

Shoghi Effendi began a similar correspondence with Dr Luṭfu'lláh Ḥakím, which continued throughout his student years. In one of his early letters to him, Shoghi Effendi communicates his own happiness and pleasure at being able to serve the Master:

> I am so glad and privileged to be able to attend to my Beloved's services after completing my course of Arts and Sciences in the American University at Beirut . . .
> The past four years have been years of untold calamity, of unprecedented oppression, of indescribable misery, of severe famine and distress, of unparalleled bloodshed and strife, but now that the dove of peace has returned to its nest and abode a golden opportunity has arisen for the promulgation of the Word of God . . . This is indeed the Era of Service.[59]

Many of the Tablets of the Master translated by Shoghi Effendi during this period of service were eventually published in *Star of the West*. For example, volume 10 of *Star of the West* reproduced Tablets of the Master translated by Shoghi Effendi for Ella Cooper and Roy Wilhelm on 12

December 1918.[60] Such Tablets were significant not only for those believers who had the bounty of receiving them but for all believers. The Tablets contained the Master's counsels and instructions for a disillusioned and confused world, counsels that were much needed at that time and are even more relevant today. The brief excerpts from some of these Tablets quoted in the next few chapters demonstrate Shoghi Effendi's developing style of English as well as convey the fragrance of the Master's words.

On 17 December 1918 Shoghi Effendi wrote from Haifa to Major Tudor-Pole attaching a translation of a Tablet the Master had written to Dr Esslemont in response to his supplication. Major Tudor-Pole acted as the trusted person in England who would distribute the messages from the Holy Land to the Bahá'ís. In his letter to Major Tudor-Pole Shoghi Effendi gave the news of the events of the day in the Holy Land. He described, for example, a meeting of the different religious heads of Haifa to institute relief work for the poor of the town. 'Abdu'l-Bahá had donated 50 Egyptian pounds for this work.[61] That same day Shoghi Effendi translated a Tablet of the Master for Mr and Mrs Vail to be sent to America.[62]

Shoghi Effendi was not known to the American Bahá'í community at this time. Dr Esslemont introduced Shoghi Effendi to the readers of the *Star of the West* in a letter published in volume 9 of that magazine:

> I was delighted to receive a copy of the translation of a Tablet which Abdul-Baha has written for me. The translation is by Shogi [sic], a grandson of the Master . . .[63]

Letters of Shoghi Effendi to Dr Ḥakím dated 19 November 1918 and to Major Tudor-Pole dated 17 December 1918 were also published in *Star of The West*; thus the American believers were introduced to this rising star in the Cause of God.[64]

The winter of 1918 was a period of intense activity for Shoghi Effendi as he translated numerous Tablets revealed by the Master. In a letter dated 26 December 1918 he describes the excitement that surrounded his heavy workload.

> Every day carries with it fresh tidings and happy news. From the Far-Eastern land, the centre of news has shifted today to Persia, in the Middle East, and thence to the extreme West in the U.S. of America. Many telegrams have arrived, and each contributed its share of consolation and solace . . .
>
> Early this morning I was ushered to His Holy presence, and there facing the Beloved on the sofa, enwrapped in His mantle with masses of supplications scattered around Him, I sat, the pen in my hand, putting down the words that flowed from His lips.[65]

The next day Shoghi Effendi translated several Tablets revealed by the Master, two of which were addressed to Tokujiro Torii and Fuyo Muchizuki in Japan and three of which were addressed to Marion Jack, Agnes Alexander and Beatrice Owens.[66] This example of Shoghi Effendi's translation of one of these Tablets, to Beatrice Owens, provides a glimpse of the Master's loving counsels to His devoted disciples:

> Every imperfect soul is self-conceited and thinks of his own good. But as his thoughts expand a little he will begin to think of the welfare and comfort of his family. If his ideas still more widen his concern will be the felicity of his fellow citizens; and if still they widen he will be thinking of the glory of his land and of his race. But when ideas and views reach the utmost degree of expansion and attain the stage of perfection then will he be interested in the exaltation of humankind. He will be then the well-wisher of all men and the seeker of the weal and prosperity of all lands. This is indicative of perfection.[67]

21

The Master's guidance to Beatrice Owens was certainly related to an inner question of hers, which this Tablet addressed, but His profound message, which is the key to the prosperity of humankind, was for all believers and for all time.

On Monday, 30 December 1918, Shoghi Effendi translated Tablets of the Master to George Latimer, Shahnaz Khanum and Jessie Revell.[68]

In a letter to Dr Luṭfu'lláh Ḥakím in London dated 7 January 1919 Shoghi Effendi explained how he spent his time from morning to evening:

> How pleased was the Beloved to receive your long letter which I immediately translated for him word by word. The Christian Commonwealth dated Dec. 4 was received to-day and the contents of the short article on the Cause duly presented to the Master . . . These days often from morn till eve have been spent in revealing tablets – and what vigorous and enthusiastic words are revealed! for America, Persia, England, India, Russia, Japan and Egypt.[69]

On January 8th and 9th eight further Tablets were translated by Shoghi Effendi, addressed to Agnes Parsons, Mrs Rasmussen, Amy Wilkinson, Isabel Chamberlain, Genevieve Coy, Anna van Blarcom, Emma Carmichael, and Alice Ives Breed.[70] Excerpts from the Tablet to Alice Ives Breed provides another example of Shoghi Effendi's developing use of English and describes the role of women in preventing war:

> If the mass of women in Europe and all those in America had been enfranchised throughout all the states, undoubtedly they would not agree to the war. At present this war has made millions of children fatherless and millions of fathers and mothers destitute of sons; this war has snatched from pitiable sisters their brethren; this war has turned millions of women widows and destitute of husbands; this war has made cities desolate; this war has brought confusion and

22

chaos in millions of villages; this war has made the very foundations of mankind quake and quiver.[71]

As the volume of supplications received from all parts of the world continued to increase, the Tablets revealed by the Master kept pace and Shoghi Effendi kept up with the translations. On 10 January he translated Tablets in honour of Zia Bagdadi, Martha Root, Geraldine Luxmore, Belle Luxmore, Henrietta Wagner, David Buchanan, Alfred Lunt and Mabel Nickerson.[72] Despite the pressure of work, a high degree of care can be seen in the translation of each Tablet. Here is an example of Shoghi Effendi's translation of the Tablet for Mabel Nickerson in which the Master reiterates the promise that divine confirmation will surround any of the friends engaged in teaching and living a Bahá'í life:

O maid-servant of His Holiness Baha'o'llah!
Thy letter dated September 25, 1918, was received. Thou hast solicited confirmation. Know thou verily that the magnet of confirmation is the promulgation of divine teachings. Whosoever arises for the diffusion of the fragrances of God, the confirmation of the Kingdom will assuredly surround him to such an extent that he will himself remain confounded.
However, this is conditioned upon the conformity of words with deeds. The people of Baha must strive to diffuse the fragrances through deeds more than through words . . .[73]

In the next few days Shoghi Effendi translated Tablets to the Assemblies of Cleveland, Santa Barbara, Akron and Urbana, to Luṭfu'lláh Ḥakím, Ella and Ellah Rice-Wray, Sarah Gertrude Harris, Isabella Brittingham and Claudia Stuart Coles, and to the Bahá'ís of the British Isles.[74]

Shoghi Effendi's work continued to increase. He produced the translations no matter how much time they took. His diligence, thoroughness and awareness of the significance of the work before him kept him at it without pause. In a letter to Dr Zia Bagdadi at this time he indicated the magnitude of his work in the service of the Master. From this letter can be seen his adaptation of a rapid, almost telegraphic style suitable for communicating information and saving time.

> To Zia M. Bagdadi, Chicago.
> Dear brother in El-Abha:
> Greetings and salutations! Your supplications are arriving; the news of the friends of God noted. A Tablet has been revealed for you; a telegram dispatched. So far, the Beloved has revealed nearly one hundred Tablets for the friends in the United States of America. Some of them have been dispatched and others will be. Convey the glad-tidings to the friends. Beloved in perfect health. Supplications and cables are pouring in constantly from morn till eve; life-giving words are revealed. From Persia, India, Japan, France, England and Switzerland, letters and telegrams are showering.[75]

During the early part of February Tablets were translated for the following individuals: Mrs J. Stannard, Elizabeth P. Hackley, Louise D. Boyle, Viola Kluge, Vitula Edith Whitton, and Corinne True.[76]

In late February 1919 Shoghi Effendi wrote to the editor of *Star of the West* enclosing a copy of a Tablet revealed by 'Abdu'l-Bahá and conveying the Master's wish that the Tablet be published in full:

> Dear Sir:-
> In accordance with the desire of our Beloved Master, enclosed herewith a copy of a Tablet that has recently been revealed to a friend in Persia which He wants you to publish fully in the Star of the West.
> > Sincerely yours,
> > Shoghi Rabbani
> > (grandson of Abdul Baha)[77]

24

Diary Letters of Shoghi Effendi, February 1919

Throughout this busy period Shoghi Effendi kept a diary of daily events in the form of letters typed by him on a manual typewriter. Multiple sheets of paper with carbon in between were used. The carbon copies convey significant information about the events that occurred during this period in the development of the Cause of God.

These letters give us an insight into the way Shoghi Effendi spent his time during the sweetest and most cherished period in his life and provide us with a fascinating picture of what it was like to be continually in the presence of 'Abdu'l-Bahá.

We know from other sources[78] that the Holy Family woke up at dawn every morning and had breakfast in the presence of the Master after the morning devotions. The stories of the Master's attention to the needs of the poor, the sick and the orphan as part of His daily routine are well known. Brief excerpts from letters written in the eleven days beginning Saturday 8 February 1919 through Tuesday 18 February 1919 describe not so much the daily routine but the significant events that occurred each day in the presence of the Master.

Saturday, 8 February 1919

This afternoon our Indian officer, Captain Agal Khan of Lahore, Punjab, who is a devout Moslem, keenly interested in the role that the Cause will play in the future . . . called on Abdul-Baha carrying with him the article of Abbas Ali of Rangoon, published in one of the local Indian papers of Punjab, which he had translated for Abdul-Baha into English. The article was a lucid and at the same time a striking account of the teachings of the Cause, of the early life, the declaration, the persecution and the martyrdom of the Bab and the rise of Baha'o'llah, his early trials, his exile, his

25

declaration and his amazing power displayed in the distant fortress of Acca.

Abdul-Baha entertained for over an hour this diligent scholar, told him that under chains and fetters Baha'o'llah propagated his teachings, the mutual arrangements of the rulers of Turkey and of Persia to quench his Light and the utter failure of their plans and intentions. Agal Khan was amazed to know that the remains of the Bab . . . were transferred to this Holy Mount . . . He resolutely decided to visit the shrine and if possible to visit the Holy Tomb in Acca.[79]

Sunday, 9 February 1919

This morning some Tablets were revealed to the friends in the United States of America. One of them . . . has written these words to Abdul-Baha: 'This humble maid-servant especially wishes to ask thee at this time, concerning the publication of two indexes . . . If this work does not interfere with carrying out the instructions already given, this maid-servant would very much like to go on and work on a complete and scholarly index of all the writings . . .

. . . Although the answer to the supplication has not yet been revealed, yet one thing is sure, that Abdul-Baha will most deeply appreciate such services and will undoubtedly breathe into their life a new breath that will sustain them throughout their activities.

This afternoon being bright and warm, Abdul-Baha ascended the mountain and visited the Tomb of the Bab where the friends had assembled for their weekly Sunday gatherings, where he inquired regarding the spiritual activities of the SPC (Beirut) to which one of its members, Mr Bahader . . . replied that their weekly Sunday gatherings are uninterruptedly held within the college grounds. This leading to a certain statement made by the president of the college with respect to his Sunday morning Bible classes, Abdul-Baha referred to the relative standing of the Holy Books and their adaptation to their respective environment. The Old Testament, he said, is largely historical and partly states various commands and regulations. The Gospel . . . reveals a whole set of admonition and exhortation, of counsels and advice. The Koran embodies all three of these and in addition reveals abstruse, scientific and mathematical problems. He then spoke in detail of the variety of the branches in mathematics and astronomy as expounded by the Egyptian, Babylonian, Greek, Roman and Persian leaders and scientists. He then referred to the rise of Ptolemy . . . He told us how all astronomers and philosophers believed in his system and although Pythagoras and Plato revealed contradictory facts, that the Ptolemaic system was considered the immutable and correct law. Then arose that illiterate, young, inexperienced Arab leader in the Arabian peninsula, who revealed in his Koran . . .: 'The sun moves in a fixed place and each star moves in its own heaven.' These bodily challenged the whole Ptolemaic system and shook it down to its very foundation . . . The whole scientific world arose to the consciousness of this truth. What clearer and stronger proof may be stated for the establishment of the truth of the Mohammedan Revelation?[80]

Monday, 10 February 1919

The misery and need of the civil population of Haifa . . . has necessitated the formation of a Haifa Relief Fund composed of the heads of the different religious denominations . . . Abdul-Baha, through the announcement made by the military governor, contributed the noble donation of £50 and inserted his name at the head of the list of contributors, which will stand as a token of his generosity, his approval of the means undertaken to alleviate the burden of the poor and his setting the noble example to the rich and leaders of the city. This morning again I was sent to the Governor and offered him a further sum for the relief of the poor. Colonel Stanton was indeed touched and, moved by this further donation, hastened to write . . . to Abdul-Baha in token of his admiration and thanks . . .

The supplications that have come today abound with refreshing news. A letter from Bombay . . . from Lausanne, Switzerland . . . from southern Palestine . . . A detailed supplication from Juanita Storch,[81] exquisitely written . . . I cannot prevent myself from sharing with you some of its charming passages:

'. . . A picture of the Master comes to me as he holds his rosary in hand out-stretched to all who heed this heavenly call. A picture of the Master comes to me as he holds his rosary, thinking of the friends both far and near as pearls of his heart. A picture of the Master comes to me as he holds his rosary, chanting in a prayerful hour, "Glory to the Most Great Power."'

To this profusion of genuine sentiments and to this authoress of tender feelings, Abdul-Baha not only spends the days in revealing his words of appreciation, but even until late at night when everything is hushed in silence and every tongue is at rest . . .

. . . As I am writing these lines, I am again moved to present myself in his presence and take down his words in response to the recently arrived supplications.[82]

Tuesday, 11 February 1919

News as contained in letters, the first since the outbreak of the war, have reached us from Persia as well as from India. Meagre and insufficient as the news is at present, yet it assures us of the welfare of the friends. Although few have succumbed to the trials and calamities occasioned by the war . . . yet consolation lies in the safety and well-being of the mass of the friends . . . In Teheren, the most active centre of Persia, the friends associate, deal and transact as Bahais, openly declaring their faith, emphatically and fearlessly delivering the message and gathering in their floor men of every class, of every denomination and of every sect – as Abdul-Baha has already repeatedly intimated in his blessed Tablets for Persia, Russia and Egypt, the only group and the one body which is able and wields the necessary power to

assure for Persia her weal and her prosperity . . . for at
present amid the agitation and uproar that still prevails in
Persia, the qualities of trustworthiness, truthfulness, obedience, frankness, conscientiousness and loyalty are exclusively
embodied in the friends of God . . .

Abdul-Baha spent the whole day indoors, with no outstanding event marking the activities of the day . . .[83]

Wednesday, 12 February 1919

This morning, some of the recently arrived supplications
were answered in the form of short yet effective Tablets. The
second supplication from India is signed by a certain influ-
ential person, a khajeh, who has been recently attracted to
the Movement and is craving to attain the court of Abdul-
Baha's presence. As emanating from a soul that has been
entangled in superstition and prejudice and immersed in
a sea of imagination, his words embodied in his supplication
are indeed significant: 'Thy generosity is the elixir and thy
bounty the solace for the weak heart of this humble servant,
and the near prospect of attaining to the holy presence
sustains his breath. O most beloved Lord, look not at the
failings, shortcomings and weakness of this humble
beseecher and entreater, but towards the boundless ocean
of thy love, mercy, bounty and grace. Grant the fervent
prayer of this humble one to approach thy holy self, keep
him not far away and separate from thee and confer upon
him the high privilege of viewing thy beautiful, illumined
face.'

. . . The Tablet revealed to this friend this morning is a
model of the sweetest and most gentle expressions that a
beloved can reveal to his loving ones.

News reaches us to the effect that the friends of God in
the different parts of Persia, devastated by famine, pesti-
lence and internecine war, have been miraculously protected
and saved . . . Letters have been received so far from Teheran, Shiraz, and tonight from Najafabad . . . However, one
thing brought gloom and depression into this lively and

clear atmosphere . . . A certain friend, buried with respect
and ceremony by his beloved and relatives, was disinterred,
his coffin was smashed to pieces, his corpse was taken out
and buried directly with no wooden case . . .[84]

Thursday, 13 February 1919

The call of Abdul-Baha bidding the friends of God to arise
in one accord, to fling away the garb of concealment and to
deliver the divine message has resounded throughout all
regions and has propagated its waves to countries hitherto
the bulwark of conservatism.

. . . This morning he [Haji Mohammed Yazdi from
Damascus] was ushered into Abdul-Baha's presence . . . With
a smile and a nod of appreciation Abdul-Baha greeted every
bit of news and was glad to know that a reaction from the
passiveness and inactivity of the past had set in. 'Deliver the
divine message with prudence and wisdom', was his recom-
mendation to the teachers who are serving in these regions.
Having said this he arose, again welcomed our guest and
regained his room to correct the Tablets that had been
revealed . . .

Abdul-Baha remained in doors until 3 P.M., when Major
Nott came and motored him to the house of the
Commander-in-chief, Sir Edmund Allenby. This was the
second time Abdul-Baha had called on the General and this
time the conversation centred around the Cause and its
progress . . . He is a very gentle, modest and striking figure,
warm in affection, yet imposing in his manners.

Tonight a telegram received . . . fixing Major Tudor-
Pole's arrival at Jerusalem on the 14th inst. and his departure on the 17th. We will be delighted to meet again this
young and active friend who is doing what he can to bring
about the comfort and the satisfaction of the Beloved.[85]

Friday, 14 February 1919

Abdul-Baha spent the whole forenoon in correcting and
signing the sixty Tablets that had been made ready during

the past days and as I am dropping you these lines he is having his fortnightly hot bath which ameliorates so much his health and strengthens his physical constitution.

Tonight we had another concrete evidence of the merit and value of Major Tudor-Pole's article in the *Palestine News*. Indeed, inquirers and seekers multiply with astonishing rapidity, a keen interest is aroused and a wide demand is being pressed more and more. The contributor of the article, Miss Hiscox in Cairo and Miss Rosenberg in London, are in correspondence with many souls, most of them in active service, who desire to learn more about the Cause than this introductory article of Major Tudor-Pole presents. Abdul-Baha was weary, tired and sleepy as a result of the heat of his bath and was intending to sleep when a slight knock at the door revealed the presence of a non-commissioned officer at the door seeking an interview. Admittance was cordially granted and there was Private Sinclair, a Britisher, working as an assistant at the Red Cross Egyptian hospital in Haifa. During his sojourn in Cairo, when visiting its reading room, he had come across Bahai literature and had thereby caught the first glimpse of the Cause. The perusal of Major Tudor-Pole's article raised his interest to its highest pitch and henceforth he became an ardent inquirer. From what could be gathered from his countenance, he was so lowly, so respectful, so gentle and so modest that the first words of the Beloved were to this effect: 'I am glad to meet thee for thy face is illumined, thy brow is pure, thy heart is clear and thy purpose is right.' . . . In view of his earnest inquiry and his lack of any preconception, the Master spoke in detail of the main purpose of the Bahai teachings, the idea of peace and reconciliation, the most immediate need of mankind. He told him of the futility of men's efforts to establish a lasting peace, resting on secure foundations, through material means. Whenever such efforts have been exerted they were doomed to failure. History affords a striking illustration. 'From what I can gather from the events during my life', said Abdul-Baha, 'history clearly shows the wars have been waged, the peace measures that were subsequently adopted, have proved inevitable failures. The Crimean war and the Treaty of Paris in 1856, the Austro-Italian war of 1859; the Danish war of 1864; the Austro-Prussian war of 1866; the Franco-Prussian war of 1870; the Russo-Turkish war of 1877; and the Congress of Berlin, the Balkan war and subsequently this world war with its present Universal Peace Conference. Wars will succeed, peace measures and pacific documents will remain dead letters unless the Word of God and His supreme power comes to exercise its influence. Not until this is attained may lasting peace be realized.'

Our attentive visitor listened and was absorbed. He was glad to listen to this remarkable talk and was furthermore grateful to receive a copy of Mr Remey's *Some Vital Bahai Principles* which Abdul-Baha put in his hands. When he retired, he was inwardly moved and outwardly satisfied and assured.[86]

Saturday, 15 February 1919

My head is in a whirl so busy and so eventful was the day. No less than a score of callers from prince and pasha to a simple private soldier have sought interview with Abdul-Baha.

Tonight again, our attracted friend, Private Sinclair of the Red Cross hospital, called. His eyes sparkled as he shook hands with the Beloved. He had read the pamphlet which had been given to him and was glad to receive another different one, published and edited by Mr Remey, entitled *The Message of Unity*. He expressed his firm intention to correspond with the different booksellers in London, as soon as he is demobilized and thus able to gather more detailed information. When he arose to take his leave, he seemed full of the spirit of Baha'o'llah, absorbed in meditation, and ablaze with His love. 'Thou art my son, my dear son, I love thee, and I pray for thee,' were the farewell words as the Beloved embraced him on his shoulders . . .

Letters, or rather parcels, were today received from Port Said, London and America. Enclosed in Mr Lotfullah's letter from London, were two supplications that had been received last year from Teheran. They contained good news. The Bahai school in Teheran is advancing by leaps and bounds. The Israelite Bahais have established schools which are rapidly widening. The school of Tarbiat in Teheran, Miss Kappes describes as by far the greatest establishment among the 430 schools in Teheran . . . In Yezd meetings of different character, each of no less than 60 to 70 attendants, were organized . . . In Yezd the maid-servants of God have risen and are overshadowing (or rather have foreshadowed) the men in their spiritual activities. Of Kashan, the writer relates, 'I had thought of it a mount of snow but later on I found it an active volcano. The friends were aflame with the fire of the Word of God.'[87]

Sunday, 16 February 1919

From among the supplications recently received is one that is most significant and of particular interest as it emanates from a Greek friend who is one of the few, if not the only of her race, that has responded to the call of the Kingdom. Let me share with you its contents: '. . . O dear Father, how could I do otherwise than believe in you because many times my mind is so tired, but when I take your picture, and I read one of your prayers, I feel just like a bird when it rains and its feathers are wet and it cannot fly, but when the sun's rays come out, is happy and flies from tree to tree – exactly I feel every minute when I make my prayers in your name. I shall not stop all my life, until I am an apostle for your name, to my people.'

. . . What the response of the Beloved will be, or rather how far the Lord's favour and blessing will surround her, is one that we can hardly venture to forecast, but one thing is sure, that the Tablet that will be revealed to this soul will act as a mighty impetus in awakening the Greek people to this call.

This morning Abdul-Baha went out for a long walk and returned an hour before noon, when he resumed his work which consisted mainly of the perusal of a detailed supplication from Persia.[88]

Monday, 17 February 1919

A day of jubilee is ahead of us. The arrival of a group of the Parsee friends of Adassieh, including men and women, has not been without a definite purpose. Another marriage festivity is to take place . . . Preparations are now being made for that day and everybody is looking forward to the celebration, the first of that kind since the extinction of the fire of war.

This morning Ágha Ahmed Yazdi, his elder brother and Ágha Mohammed Taghi Esfahani were called to the Beloved's presence. Tea was served and everybody assumed almost an uninterrupted silence for Abdul-Baha was throughout perusing supplications of the Egyptian friends, who had recently arrived. Supplications from every corner of the globe, of different length and character, written in different languages, enclosing clippings of papers, pamphlets, typewritten reports, petitions, etc., are ceaselessly pouring in and the time for their perusal is sufficient to exhaust all the time that one might possibly have at his disposal. Although the ways have not yet fully opened and communication with all parts has not yet been restored, one is baffled at the amount of letters, books and magazines that the postoffice daily delivers.

A letter from Mirza Mahmood Zarkani from Bombay to Haji Mirza Haider Ali reveals the great longing of the Parsee friends to met Abdul-Baha, whether in the Holy Land or in India.[89]

Tuesday, 18 February 1919

Greetings with sweetest remembrances to you . . . from this hallowed spot! From this solitary plain of Bahjeh, in this solemn solitude, away from life's tumult and bustle, I take the pen . . . The Beloved has again decided to tarry for a time at the vicinity of the tomb of his father. Here he is, in the adjoining room, sitting by the candle light, viewing from his window the solitude from afar, the silent surroundings, which nothing breaks save the distant roar of the waves which die away in the immensity of space. He is engaged in his meditations, absorbed in his prayers, thinking of his friends across the seas, remembering their prayers and their supplications and communing with his heavenly Father on behalf of such souls. What a vivid contrast does this vicinity of the Holy Tomb represent with the increasing activity of the life in Haifa. The air over there was filled with gases and vapours which steam and motor engines continuously discharge, while the atmosphere here is as pure, as clear and as fragrant as it can be. The traffic accompanied with its deafening noise and bustle, gives way here to a stillness, a calmness and a quietude which nothing interrupts but the stillness of nature. The dazzling lights of the city are gone and nothing but a flickering taper's light cheers this cold and starless night. The constant movement and circulation witnessed in the Beloved's house has stopped, and tonight everything is at a stand still, everything quiet and at rest. The morning hour of prayer is maintained and even lengthened for twice a day, the Beloved visits the Holy shrine, kneels in reverence and devotion, orders communes to be chanted and often spends an hour or more in silent prayer. His attendants, friends and relatives are absent and no one save Kosro, Esfandiar and myself, the two vigilant guardians of the Tomb, and Ali Eff, a friend who will leave tomorrow for Beirut, form his small retinue.

Everything, the environment, the atmosphere, the view, the stillness, all are uplifting, elevating and inspiring. One feels to have forgotten his cares and his concerns, his mind is refreshed and his burden alleviated. No matter how long the Master will tarry in this sanctified place, no feeling of monotony, and ennui overcomes the soul. It is the Spot which so many souls crave to attain and long to visit. Particularly is it magnificent at such a time when nature is smiling, the sky above is no more gloomy and threatening with clouds but serene and blue, the plains and meadows as if covered with a multicoloured carpet, the shrubs sparkling with roses, jasmines, lilies, narcissus embalming the pure and refreshing air; the grass growing luxuriously everywhere and the breeze wafting in every direction. Often is the Beloved seen in the open air, majestically walking to and fro upon the verdant plains and amid the wild flowers that abound in this gifted region. He treads the same ground that the blessed feet of his heavenly Father have trodden, circumambulates the shrine where for many years He has lived, waters the flowers and plants, many of which have been blessed by His hands and lives and moves and has his being in an atmosphere which fully reminds him of His manners and His conduct. What a dear and blessed spot to be privileged to live in![90]

4

In the Service of the Master
Spring 1919

During the spring of 1919 the pressure of work on translations decreased, allowing Shoghi Effendi to direct his attention to correspondence. This included his own correspondence, as well as letters he wrote conveying the Master's wishes to the friends throughout the world. His translation work did not, however, completely cease. On 15 March 1919 Shoghi Effendi translated Tablets of the Master for Louise Waite and Olive Couch.[91] The Tablet to Louise Waite conveys the significance of the Covenant of God and assures the friends that the damage caused by those who break the Covenant will not endure. A paragraph from the Tablet to Louise Waite describes the fortune of Covenant-breakers:

> Ere long thou shalt consider that no sign and no trace shall remain therefrom. The ocean of the Covenant shall send forth a wave and shall disperse and throw out these foams.[92]

Concurrent with the sad news of the activities of the Covenant-breakers, the news of the dedication, steadfastness and services of the believers reached the Holy Land. Corinne True, who will always be remembered for her services in furthering the construction of the Mother Temple of the West, had sent a supplication to the Master with news of the devoted services of the friends. In a letter to her dated Monday, 17 March 1919, Shoghi Effendi expresses his happiness with the news of her dedication and conveys his appreciation of her glorious services to the Cause and her keen interest in the Bahá'í temple.

In this same letter Shoghi Effendi writes of 'Abdu'l-Bahá's untiring efforts to promote Bahá'u'lláh's teachings:

> The Beloved from morn till eve, even at midnight is engaged in revealing Tablets, in sending forth his constructive, dynamic thoughts of love and principles to a sad and distracted world. In most of the Tablets he lays great stress upon unity, love and firmness in the Covenant.[93]

On the same day, Shoghi Effendi translated Tablets of the Master to Jean Masson and Dorothy Nelson.[94] A paragraph from the Tablet to Jean Masson is typical of the Master's repeated reminders to His steadfast band of followers of His earnest hopes for their spiritual advancement and provides an example of Shoghi Effendi's translation skills at this time:

> My hope is that day by day thou mayest be more confirmed and may serve to the best the world of humanity; that thou mayest adore mankind and ignite in every heart the lamp of guidance, may serve the world of morality so that human realities may be freed from the gloom of the world of nature which, in essence, is purely animal in character, and may be illumined with the light of the divine realm.[95]

With a letter to *Star of the West* written on the same day, Shoghi Effendi enclosed a Tablet of the Master revealed to the 'friends and the maid-servants of the Merciful in the country of Egypt'. He indicated that it was the wish of 'Abdu'l-Bahá that the Tablet be published in *Star of the West*. This Tablet, published in both English and Arabic, expresses the Master's praise and gratitude to God for the bounties He has bestowed upon humanity through this glorious revelation. The English translation was made by Dr Zia Bagdadi.[96]

38

On 30 March Shoghi Effendi translated the Master's Tablets to Edna True and Mrs Brooker.[97] To Mrs Brooker the Master expressed His good pleasure at the meeting she had organized for teaching the Cause:

> Praise thou the Lord, that thou hast been ushered into the divine Kingdom as one of the chosen people of God and the light of guidance hath been reflected upon thy pure heart . . . thou hast organized a meeting and hast been engaged in the promulgation of divine teachings.
>
> Rest thou assured that divine confirmations shall reach (thee) . . .[98]

On Friday, 4 April 1919 Shoghi Effendi translated a Tablet for Juliet Thompson in which the Master calls upon her to detach herself from the world of nature and become 'God-like, Lordly, illumined and merciful'. He also asks her to convey His greetings to Kahlil Gibran.[99]

On Friday, 11 April Shoghi Effendi translated Tablets for the Cleveland Assembly, Elizabeth Herlitz and Mr and Mrs Richter.[100] This excerpt is from the Tablet to the Cleveland Assembly, addressed to 'the children of the Kingdom':

> My highest wish and desire is that ye who are my children may be educated according to the teachings of His Holiness Baha'o'llah and may receive a Bahai training; that ye may each become an ignited candle of the world of humanity, may be devoted to the service of all mankind, may give up your rest and comfort, so that ye may become the cause of the tranquillity of the world of creation.[101]

Such inspiring counsels revealed by 'Abdu'l-Bahá and translated by Shoghi Effendi continued to stream forth from the pen of the Centre of the Covenant. They covered a wide range of topics raised by the believers in the East and the West and touched the hearts of their recipients. They served as a beacon of light to a confused and distracted world, calling it to a higher plane of existence and raising aloft high standards of conduct and service to humanity.

The Master's plea to each group was directed to the situation and the needs of that group. For example, in a Tablet to Howard MacNutt translated by Shoghi Effendi on Sunday 13 April 1919, 'Abdu'l-Bahá encouraged the friends to write papers that communicate the Bahá'í teachings and to present them in meetings with brilliancy and eloquence:

> At present, like unto the morn, the lights of the Sun of Truth have been shed around. Effort must be made that the slumbering souls may be awakened, the heedless become vigilant, and the divine instructions, which constitute the spirit of this age, may reach the ears of the people of the world, may be propagated in papers and enunciated in meetings with the utmost brilliancy and eloquence.[102]

A letter dated 25 April 1919 written by Shoghi Effendi to Dr Zia Bagdadi is a general communication to the Bahá'í world reminiscent, in retrospect, of the messages he would send to the Bahá'í world at a later period of his guardianship, as these two paragraphs demonstrate:

> News, refreshing and inspiring, is being daily received from all over the world, from the far west in the United States of America to the middle east in Persia and the far east, Japan and India, and still beyond from the Hawaiian islands in the mid-Pacific ocean. From New Zealand even the glad tidings of the Kingdom are breaking upon us and indicate the brilliant future that is stored for the far-off continent of Australia . . .
>
> What strikes us most vividly is the good news of the welfare and safety of the friends of God. All throughout the years of war, civil as well as national, of loot and of riot and rebellion and of bloodshed, the friends have been continuously engaged in service to the Cause of God. Their

meetings have not been discontinued, their fervour has not decreased and their energy has not relaxed.[103]

The next day, 26 April, Shoghi Effendi translated Tablets for Joseph Hannen and Roy Wilhelm.[104] In the Tablet to Roy Wilhelm the Master reiterates the futility of the efforts of the Covenant-breakers.

On Thursday, 8 May 1919 Shoghi Effendi wrote from Haifa to Dr Luṭfu'lláh Ḥakím, giving him the news that the annual consultative Bahá'í Convention of the friends in India and Burma was being planned for the coming Christmas. He stated that the friends in India were active in the service of the Cause and were hoping that their services would draw 'Abdu'l-Bahá to their shores.[105]

The Master received a joint supplication bearing the signature of a thousand believers in America and Canada inviting Him to visit America again.[106] On 22 May 1919 Shoghi Effendi wrote to Ahmad Sohrab, who had left for America on 23 December via Cairo and Liverpool, enclosing a Tablet from the Master for the Bahá'í friends in America and Canada in response to their loving supplications and invitation. Here is an excerpt from Shoghi Effendi's letter:

> The clock is striking ten, and having just returned to the Beloved's own sleeping room on the terrace of Abbas Kuli's house which lies only a few steps east of the Tomb of the Bab, I remembered my friends in the East and therefore resume at this period of the night my correspondence with them. In view of the repeated attacks of malaria that I have been subjected to, the Beloved ordered me to pass a few nights on Mount Carmel in the vicinity of the Tomb, enjoying the pure invigorating and spiritual atmosphere of Makam . . . such a lovely and silent scene would have long detained me outside had it not been for my keen desire to share with my spiritual brethren and sisters the contents of a general Tablet, the first of its kind since the resumption of communication and addressed to all the friends and

41

maid-servants of God throughout the United States of America and Canada.[107]

In His Tablet the Master showered His love on the believers of the United States of America and Canada and called them to attain higher levels of unity and concord, as in this excerpt:

> Ye are inviting me to America. I am likewise longing to gaze at those illumined faces and converse and associate with those real friends. But the magnetic power which shall draw me to those shores is the union and harmony of the friends, their behaviour and conduct in accordance with the teachings of God and the firmness of all in the Covenant and the Testament.[108]

The idea of writing the supplication to 'Abdu'l-Bahá which attracted this remarkable Tablet had been born at a Feast held on 16 October 1918 in the home of Mrs Leo Perron in Chicago. The idea was discussed at the meeting of the House of Spirituality, where it was suggested that all the friends in the country could join in an act of unity and send a joint supplication to the Master. The secretary was instructed to address all the assemblies and put the matter before them. Miss Jean Masson, assisted by a committee, drafted the supplication. The signatures were received over several weeks and in the early part of January 1919 the entire document was sent to 'Akká.[109]

5

In the Service of the Master
Summer 1919

By the summer of 1919 Shoghi Effendi was a youth of 22. One year had elapsed since his graduation from the American University of Beirut and commencing his work of service to the Master. His entire learning and scholarly discipline had been channelled into the work of translation and correspondence. Yet Shoghi Effendi's contribution went far beyond these twin tasks. Looking back at this period in the history of the Faith, it is remarkable to see the two figures into whose care the Cause of God was successively entrusted – 'Abdu'l-Bahá, the Centre of the Covenant, and Shoghi Effendi, its future Guardian – working together at the centre of the Bahá'í world.

The work of Shoghi Effendi during this period continued on the same path, sometimes with a heavier concentration on translation and sometimes on correspondence.

In his diary letter of Sunday, 8 June 1919, Shoghi Effendi refers to a gathering that day in the presence of the Master around the shrine of Bahá'u'lláh at which one of the Persian friends gave a description of the Bahá'í House of Worship in Ishqábád. The Master referred to the uniqueness of this House of Worship, the first of its kind to be erected to the praise of God, and remarked that the 'Temple that is going to be erected in the United States will be an important and magnificent one, its influence and reaction upon the Cause will be tremendous, and the impetus it shall give to the movement, irresistible'.[110]

Such clear guidance and vision regarding the House of Worship in North America communicated that day by the Master would emerge years later in the form of repeated messages from the Guardian of the Faith encouraging the friends to complete the Mother Temple of the West.

The precious period when Shoghi Effendi served the Master was indeed filled with excitement. Letters giving news of the progress of the Cause and the devotion of the friends were pouring in every day. As mentioned above, one such letter was the joint supplication of the believers in the United States and Canada bearing over a thousand signatures. This supplication brought great joy to the heart of the Master. On Wednesday, 11 June 1919 Shoghi Effendi wrote from 'Akká to Dr Zia Bagdadi stating that a remarkable Tablet had been revealed by the Master 'for the friends and maid-servants of God throughout the United States and Canada'. He stated that he was enclosing the Tablet along with the supplication and the names of those who had signed it. In his note Shoghi Effendi conveys the specific instructions of the Master about the publication of these important documents:

Abdu'l-Baha ordered me to write to you concerning this important, momentous question. Publish in the Persian and English columns of the Star of the West the Persian and English texts of the enclosed supplication. Then publish all the names one by one and after that publish the general Tablet in Persian as well as in English, all in the same copy of the Star, no matter how voluminous it may become. Then send at least a couple of copies to every province in Persia, addressed to Bahai Assemblies or individuals. Also send at least one copy of the convention photo to each province of Persia, that all Persian Bahais may see what miracles have been wrought, what achievements have been made, what victories have been won, what a universal, a simultaneous response to the trumpet call of service has taken hold of the western friends. This is the Beloved's command, fulfil it . . .[111]

This letter conveys the instructions of the Master in a style intended by Him. It is clear that the decision about how much of the material to publish was made by the Master, His wishes in the matter being communicated clearly and unmistakably by Shoghi Effendi.

The American friends had been busy drafting the joint supplication to the Master during the winter and in January of 1919. Therefore many people had not sent individual letters to Him. By the summer, however, having already sent the joint supplication, the friends resumed writing their individual supplications.

In his letter of 12 June to Dr Esslemont, Shoghi Effendi refers to the increase in the volume of supplications:

Supplications are flooding and pouring out incessantly. Mighty and numerous are the Tablets revealed every day. Often I am kept working at my desk and translating Tablets till past midnight. But still I am happy and grateful . . .[112]

The Master continued to reveal Tablets in answer to these supplications. On 24 June Shoghi Effendi translated Tablets addressed to the Executive Board of Bahá'í Temple Unity, to Harlan Foster Ober and Agnes Leo.[113]

In the midst of his translation work Shoghi Effendi found time to write to Dr Esslemont, from whom he had not heard for some time, enclosing a few pages of his diary:

It is a long time that I have been deprived of the pleasure & privilege of reading your lovely letters and I hope you will soon interrupt this silence & will assure us of your safety and welfare . . .[114]

During the month of July 1919 the volume of translations continued to increase. On Wednesday, 16 July, Shoghi Effendi translated Tablets for Jessie Revell, Maria Rebecca Robertson, and Maud Thompson.[115] On Friday, 18 July, he translated Tablets addressed to Helen Whitney, Edgar Waite, Ollie James Watts and J.E. Gilligan, Sarah Van Winkle, Amy Williams, Ernest Walters and Norma Wilson.[116] On Sunday, 20 July, an additional ten Tablets were translated addressed to John Wolcott, Mr and Mrs Latimer, Sophie Loeding, Edward Struven, James Simpson, Elizabeth Stevens, Ferdinand Peterson, Martha Root, Ella Quant and Mr and Mrs Scheffler.[117] Two days later, on Tuesday, 22 July, again Shoghi Effendi translated ten Tablets, to Mary Lesch, Mary Morrison, Fruitport Assembly, L.B. Nash, Peter Maus, Emily Olsen, James Morton, the Racine Assembly, Alfred Lunt and Jean Masson.[118]

On Thursday, 23 July, Shoghi Effendi continued to undertake translations, with Tablets to Mr and Mrs Beckett, Mother Beecher and to the Bahá'ís of California.[119] The next day, on 24 July 1919, Shoghi Effendi translated Tablets to Corinne True, Louis Gregory, Kokab MacCutcheon and Mr and Mrs Howard MacNutt.[120] On Friday, 25 July, two Tablets were translated, for Ruth Klos and William F. Kyle.[121] The next day, 26 July, Shoghi Effendi translated four Tablets, for Mr and Mrs Gift, Oscar Hanko, Mary Hall and Dr Pauline Barton-Peeke.[122] On 29 July Tablets for the Bahá'ís of Central States and Gertrude Buikema were translated[123] and on Wednesday, 30 July, Shoghi Effendi translated a Tablet of the Master for Agnes Alexander.[124]

These Tablets, translated during the month of July, conveyed the love of the Master to His disciples and contained His response to each supplication. Some were brief while others were quite lengthy. Some conveyed the Master's pleasure at the spiritual atmosphere of the recent convention, as in this Tablet to Ferdinand Peterson:

Shoghi Effendi in the service of the Master, circa 1919

Shoghi Effendi, seated second from the right, with the Master and Bahá'ís in the Holy Land

Shoghi Effendi is introduced to the American Bahá'í community

Shoghi Effendi with the Master, February 1919

Shoghi Effendi, seated third from the right, among the believers in Alexandria in 1920, prior to his departure for Europe

Shoghi Effendi, standing to the left of 'Abdu'l-Bahá, in Haifa, 2 October 1919

Shoghi Effendi in the oriental dress he often wore before leaving the Holy Land to study in England

Neuilly-sur-Seine,
6 Bd. du Château,
11 June 1920.

Dear Sir;

My esteemed friend, Sir Herbert Samuel, advises me to write you inquiring about admission as a non-collegiate student at Balliol College or any other college at Oxford University.

My sole aim is to perfect my English, to acquire the literary ability to write it well & translate correctly & fluently from Persian & Arabic into English. My aim is to concentrate for two years upon this object & to acquire it through the help of a tutor, by attending lectures, by associating with cultured & refined literary circles & by receiving intensive instruction in rhetoric.

I would be much obliged if you could help me along that line.

Yours very sincerely,
Shoghi Rabbani.

Shoghi Effendi's letter of application to Balliol College, Oxford

Thou hadst written that this year thou hast attended the Convention, hast been present at that illumined assemblage, hast heard those merciful addresses, hast secured a fresh spirit and hast increased in faith, assurance and firmness in the Covenant. Appreciate the value of this lordly bounty and thank God that thou art living in the dispensation of the Covenant, and art attracted to the Sun of the Reality of the Abha Beauty – May my life be a sacrifice to His friends![125]

Another theme of the Tablets translated by Shoghi Effendi during the month of July is Covenant-breaking in response to reports of the activities of the Covenant-breakers. While the Master's love surrounded both the friends and the enemies of the Cause, He warned the friends of the personal motives and intentions of the violators of the Covenant and made it clear that the only power that can unite the world is the power of the Covenant. Questioning the power of the Covenant is the same as questioning one's belief in the principle of oneness. In the Tablet to Martha Root the Master referred to the Covenant-breakers:

. . . these souls are themselves at present among the pioneers of violation. This is because of their personal motives for they had thought of securing leadership and wealth, but when they considered that in remaining firm in the Covenant their purpose would not be realized, they deviated from it. Those souls must have been either at first truthful and now disloyal or at first disloyal and now truthful. At any rate their lie is manifest. Notwithstanding this, some souls who are not aware of this fact waver when those cast the seeds of suspicion. Awaken all the people and send a copy of this letter to Mr Remey, Mrs Goodall and Mrs Cooper.[126]

Among the Tablets translated during this month by Shoghi Effendi is one to Alfred Lunt, which contained the Master's words of wisdom on a different theme:

The essence of the Bahai economic teachings is this, that immense riches far beyond what is necessary should not be accumulated. For instance, the well-known Morgan, who possessed a sum of three hundred millions, and was day and night restless and agitated, did not partake of the divine bestowals save a little broth. This wealth was for him a vicissitude and not the cause of comfort.

He invited me to his library and to his home that I might visit the former and have dinner at his house. I went to the library in order to look at the Oriental books, but did not go to his house, and did not accept his invitation. In short, he eagerly desired that I should visit him in the library but meanwhile important financial problems arose which prevented him from being present, and thus he was deprived of this bounty. Now, had he not such excessive amount of wealth, he might have been able to present himself.[127]

Diary Letters of Shoghi Effendi, August 1919

Shoghi Effendi continued to write his diary letters through the summer of 1919. The summaries of these letters, provided below, give a flavour of his experiences in the presence of the Master. Again, it is not so much the daily routine in the life of the Master that Shoghi Effendi records but the significant events.[128]

Sunday, 3 August 1919

This day was eventful. The Master made several significant statements. He revealed a Tablet for the ex-governor of New York City in which He presented the basic teachings of the Faith and praised the humanitarian actions of the government officials.

Consul Abelia, who had been in charge of British interests in Haifa, came to visit the Master. The Master spoke to this visitor about the oppression and misery in the region during the war.

Before noon more visitors, the deputy governor of 'Akká and his wife, came to see 'Abdu'l-Bahá. The conversation centred topics that interested the deputy governor including social reconstruction, the industrial crisis, the spread of Bolshevism and so on. The deputy governor and his wife had lunch with the Master during which 'Abdu'l-Bahá spoke of the sacredness of Mount Carmel and the unique position of the Shrine of the Báb. At two o'clock the deputy governor and the Master were driven to the Shrine of the Báb. There, near the middle gate facing 'Akká, they sat and discussed the spiritual significance of Carmel.

In the afternoon, after the deputy governor and his wife had gone, Mrs Stannard, the friends and pilgrims arrived. They sat in the presence of the Master and listened to His important discourse. Mrs Stannard said to the Master that she was happy to see Him so comfortable. In response, the Master said:

> I have always felt at rest. Hast thou ever seen me uncomfortable? It does not make any difference to me. Do you want me to tell you the truth? At a time when I was confined, I felt much more comfortable and was much happier . . .

4–9 August 1919

Owing to the pressure of work comprising the transcription, translation and dispatch of Tablets as well as the perusal of a great number of supplications addressed to the Master from Europe and America, Shoghi Effendi had to discontinue his daily notes and summarize the events of the week. He wrote:

> Piles of supplications await His immediate consideration while His communications and Tablets which have reached

49

the proportion of booklets have to be immediately revised, translated and transcribed. Telegrams are pouring in every day from different parts of the globe and newspaper reports and clippings, books and pamphlets add a great deal to the amount of mail that is being conveyed every day.

Major Moore, a British officer and correspondent for the *Times of Teheran* came to see 'Abdu'l-Bahá. This officer, an ardent proponent of the League of Nations, received the Master's vision for the future of this body and its evolution towards an effective world organization. The Master spoke further about how the war had shown the need for peace. War, He said, is not a means for acquiring power. Far greater results are possible through unity: scientific achievements employed for war can be used for peace and human faculties can serve to accelerate the movement towards peace.

Sunday, 10 August 1919

Major Moore came again in the morning to see 'Abdu'l-Bahá and to ask two questions. First, he wanted to know what effect prayer and concentration have on those who are the subject of concentration and how one acquires the condition of prayer – the state of ecstasy. Second, he wished to know the nature and text of Bahá'u'lláh's prophecies.

The Master's answer to the first question was that man cannot stimulate and awaken others if he is speechless and inactive. His prayer can only bring a change through divine power. However, as soon as the person puts his thoughts into action his hearers can be inspired.

Regarding the condition of prayer, the Master said that the best time for prayer is at dawn and dusk. The power of will draws one to the condition of prayer. When one is not in a receptive mood and is rather immersed in one's worldly affairs, he can pull himself into the condition of prayer by an act of will:

By a force of will and an effort of mind, man turns his attention to God, to His knowledge, His wonderful creation, His wisdom and His Omnipotence, and then by thinking frequently and deeply of Him, attains the state of Love, of desire for prayer, of supreme ecstacy. But sometimes one finds that Divine power and not human effort transports man into that condition.

Regarding Major Moore's second question, the Master said that Bahá'u'lláh's prophecies were published some 30 years earlier in India, Persia and Egypt. He asked for a copy of two books to be brought to Him from which He read in a thrilling voice. From the Kitáb-i-Aqdas He read prophecies referring to:

. . .the fall of Abdul-Hamid, the oppression and misrule that raised high their head in Constantinople, the cry of the Owl which is heard from the people of Turkey, the collapse of Germany, the sudden fall of the King of Berlin, the lamentations again of Berlin and the promising and bright future that lies ahead of Teheran particularly and the whole of Persia generally.

A carbon copy of this set of diary letters was sent to Dr Esslemont on Monday, 11 August 1919. In the cover letter Shoghi Effendi wrote of his anticipation of Esslemont's visit in October:

My dear, dear Dr Esslemont:
    Your kind letter enclosing your most welcomed portrait was received. Dear Lotfullah who arrived safely delivered it to me and I was glad to hear your news and those of the friends in England. As soon as your supplication & photograph was presented by dear Lotfullah, a lovely Tablet was revealed for you which shall be duly forwarded. The Beloved is in the best health & pilgrims are pouring in from the four distant corners of the globe. Now we all look forward to

51

meet you, safe & healthy this coming October! As I have no good single picture of my own, I send you a grey picture taken recently in the vicinity of the tomb of the Bab, wherein I am marked with a cross on the sleeves.

I enclose for you some recent copies of my diary which include some of the interesting talks & remarkable declarations of the Beloved. I must gladden your heart, as I know how anxious you are, of the good health & happiness of the Master. He is feeling indeed very well and is exceedingly busy.

I am well and glad to have met Lotfullah, whom I meet daily and with whom yesterday I had a lovely walk in moonlight on Carmel. I hope to meet you there in October & pass with you a long time in perfect joy & fragrance.

I am ever your friend,

Shoghi

6

Last Months with the Master

The time of separation from the Master was fast approaching. The seven-month period between mid-August 1919 and early spring 1920 comprised the last fleeting months Shoghi Effendi was in the presence of 'Abdu'l-Bahá.

At the beginning of this period Shoghi Effendi was separated also from his college friends from the American University of Beirut. The group of Persian students who had attended the University was dispersing. Many were now leaving for Europe. Among these students was Ali Yazdi, a college friend of Shoghi Effendi. On 24 August 1919 Shoghi Effendi wrote about the scattering of this group in his diary.

> This week has been, viewed from one aspect, a sad and depressing one. It has witnessed the scattering of friends who during the war and prior to it have been for years held closely and affectionately together by bonds of fellowship and common interest. The student Bahá'í group at the American University – that company of young, brilliant, active, and upright men, which has all throughout the war retained, notwithstanding its vicissitudes and blows, its cohesion, is now splitting up, its numbers mostly graduates of that university departing from that common centre . . . Mr 'Alí Yazdí is just starting from Damascus to Haifa where, after meeting with the Beloved, he will proceed to Berlin to engage in higher studies.
>
> Sad has been the farewell . . . but the idea that these young men, enlightened and active as they are, may one day each in his own sphere of action render a service to the

53

Cause, affords sufficient consolation for the hearts that remain behind.[129]

Ali Yazdi left Haifa by train to go to Port Said where he was to take the ship to Switzerland and Germany. Shoghi Effendi saw him off at the station in Haifa. He sat in the compartment until the train was ready to leave; then he said good-bye and asked Ali Yazdi to write to him. During the next two years the two friends kept up a correspondence and met in Oxford.

In his own sphere of action, Shoghi Effendi's services to the Cause continued with the same intensity as before, translating for the Master and serving the distinguished visitors and pilgrims who came to see 'Abdu'l-Bahá during this period. *Star of the West* published two Tablets he translated in August 1919, one addressed to Louise Smith, translated on 2 August, and the other to Emma B. Stott, translated on August 27.[130]

Star of the West contains no Tablets translated by Shoghi Effendi in September. This does not mean that Shoghi Effendi stopped translating Tablets or that he had reduced his translation work. Many Tablets he translated for the friends during this period were never published. Of the Tablets translated by Shoghi Effendi in October, two were published in *Star of the West*, one for Flora Clark on 13 October and the other for H. De Boer on 14 October.[131]

There is one Tablet in *Star of the West* translated by Shoghi Effendi during November 1919. This Tablet, addressed to Mrs Carpenter and translated on 12 November, demonstrates the love of the Master for His disciples:

. . . I am writing thee in brief that thou mayest know that thou art ever within sight and present before me.

I beg for thee from the bounties of God advancement in the Kingdom and nearness to His Highness the Merciful One.[132]

'Abdu'l-Bahá's love surrounded His disciples in the East and the West. The believers were invigorated by His Tablets and strived constantly to attain His good pleasure and to go on pilgrimage to see Him. One of these believers was Dr Esslemont. He had received many Tablets from the Master and was granted permission to go on pilgrimage. His eagerly anticipated arrival in the Holy Land occurred in December 1919.

Shoghi Effendi was anxious to meet this friend with whom he had corresponded during the previous year. On 8 December 1919 Dr Esslemont joined Shoghi Effendi on a visit to 'Akká together with Dr Ḥakím and Isfandíyár, 'Abdu'l-Bahá's servant. The close relationship between Shoghi Effendi and Dr Esslemont was consolidated during this pilgrimage.[133]

On Tuesday, 9 December 1919 Shoghi Effendi wrote to Ali Yazdi to develop further the friendship that had evolved from childhood:

My dearest 'Alí

For a long time have I awaited your letters as I was in the dark as to your whereabouts. But now that your father has come for a few days from Damascus, I secured your address and am sending you herewith some news of the Holy Land.

The Beloved is in the best health and so are the friends and pilgrims. Your dear and devoted father is as ever warm-hearted, loving, rosy-cheeked, and in full bloom. Your brother is studying at SPC and all runs smoothly. I was told last night that he is growing wonderfully in height and his studies above par.

As to myself, the same work and the same room.

So please write me and forget me not as I do not and cannot forget the dear Sheikh!

Yours affectionately

Shoghi[134]

Shoghi Effendi wrote again to Ali Yazdi on Wednesday, 17 December enclosing a Tablet of the Master addressed to the German friends:

> Dearest 'Alí!
>
> Your letter from Stuttgart dated Nov. 27 is at hand. I exposed its content to the Master, and I secured this Tablet for you in his own handwriting addressed to the German friends. I herewith enclose it.
>
> Your dear father is here, and we exchange the news of your letters to me and to him. He is well and happy. I trust you have received my letter to you dated Dec. 8, which I sent to the Technische Hochschule and in which I enclosed some diary letters of mine which I thought might interest you.
>
> We are exceedingly busy here. Some fifty pilgrims, Arabs, Kurds, Persians, Americans, Europeans, and Japanese.[135]

On 17 December 1919 we see the beginning of collaborative translations of Shoghi Effendi, translations where he secured the assistance of several individuals. A significant Tablet, revealed by the Master to the people of the world, was translated jointly by Shoghi Effendi, Dr Zia Bagdadi, Luṭfu'lláh Ḥakím and Dr Esslemont:

> O people of the World!
>
> The dawn of the Sun of Reality is assuredly for the illumination of the world and for the manifestation of mercy. In the assemblage of the family of Adam results and fruits are praiseworthy, and the holy bestowals of every bounty are abundant . . .
>
> Then, O ye friends of God! Appreciate the value of this precious Revelation, move and act in accordance with it and walk in the straight path and the right way. Show it to the people. Raise the melody of the Kingdom and spread abroad the teachings and ordinances of the loving Lord so that the world may become another world, the darkened

56

earth may become illumined and the dead body of the people may obtain new life . . .[136]

On 24 December 1919 Shoghi Effendi translated Tablets for Charles Mason Remey and Marie Watson.[137] On Thursday, 25 December 1919, as a token of his friendship with Dr Esslemont, Shoghi Effendi presented him with a precious gift and this message:

> The rarest, dearest, & most precious treasure that Shoghie [sic] could give to his unforgettable friend Dr Esslemont – a drop of the coagulated & sacred blood of Baha'ullah . . .[138]

Shoghi Effendi's strong desire and determination to serve the Cause and his sense of the urgency of the hour imposed on him a discipline that ignored his comfort and health. While at the Syrian Protestant College he had endeavoured to excel by learning as much as he could in preparation for his service. When he began his service to the Master he put the work of the Cause before his own rest and comfort, working well into the night with little rest during this entire period. The two spells of intense translation activity caused by increases in 'Abdu'l-Bahá's correspondence just after the end of the war and after the 1919 American convention put much pressure upon the youthful figure of Shoghi Effendi and weakened his health. He was also subjected to repeated attacks of malaria in the spring of 1919. The effect of this illness and his lack of rest on the one hand and his intense desire to do his utmost to render a worthy service to the Master on the other damaged his health to the extent that he needed rest and treatment.

As early as 23 January 1920 the translations published in *Star of the West* were rendered by Azizullah Bahadur and other individuals such as Luṭfu'lláh Ḥakím and Ahmad Sohrab. However, Shoghi Effendi continued to translate Tablets of the Master for the friends in Britain.

7

Recuperation in Paris

'Abdu'l-Bahá, concerned about the health of His beloved grandson, insisted that Shoghi Effendi spend some time in rest and recuperation. He chose the sanatorium in Neuilly, a suburb of Paris, for this purpose and arranged for Shoghi Effendi to go there accompanied by Dr Luṭfu'lláh Ḥakím.[139] Shoghi Effendi entered *Maison d'Hydrothérapie et de convalescence du Parc de Neuilly*, located at 6 Boulevard du Château, in Neuilly-sur-Seine, in April 1920.

In an undated letter written from Neuilly to Ali Kuli Khan in Paris, Shoghi Effendi stated that his physical health was improving and his nerves were consolidated while still under treatment. He hoped that he would soon completely recover, as this would bring joy and assurance to the heart of the beloved Master. He asked Ali Kuli Khan to please inform him of any news from the Holy Land, as such news brought tranquillity to his heart. Shoghi Effendi stated that he would miss seeing Ali Kuli Khan that evening when he planned to visit his family.[140]

Ali Kuli Khan was a devoted believer who had served the Master as interpreter during His visit to the United States and had arranged interviews for the Master when he served as Chief Diplomatic Representative and Chargé d'Affaires at the Persian Embassy in Washington. After the war he was sent to Paris as a member of the Persian Delegation to the Versailles Peace Conference and was living in Paris.[141]

On Sunday, 25 April 1920 Shoghi Effendi wrote another letter from Neuilly to Ali Kuli Khan, who was on a visit to

London, sending him his most joyous and fondest Bahá'í greetings and thanking him for his letter that was filled with kindness, faithfulness, devotion and love. He gave Ali Kuli Khan the good news that, by the grace of God, the blessings of the beloved Master and the loving care that Ali Kuli Khan had provided him, his health had ameliorated and with divine assistance he would soon recover completely. He hoped to visit Ali Kuli Khan's home within one or two weeks and spend some time with him in an atmosphere of spiritual companionship. Meanwhile, in accordance with the wishes of the Master and the instructions of the doctor, he was spending the mornings till noon in his room, sometimes sitting in bed and other times busily writing and copying certain Tablets. In the afternoons he went for walks outside the sanitorium. It was the wish of 'Abdu'l-Bahá, he said, that he should wear a hat, and since his hat was worn out, he sought Ali Kuli Khan's guidance in acquiring a Persian hat in Paris.[142]

On Saturday, 8 May 1920 Shoghi Effendi sent a postcard from Neuilly to Ali Yazdi in which he described his state of health:

Dearest 'Alí!

I have not forgotten you, but do you know and realize what crisis I have passed and into what state of health I have fallen! For a month I have stayed and am still staying in this 'maison de convalescence' away from Paris and its clamour in bed until noon, receiving . . . treatment and following the Master's instructions not to open a book during my stay in this place. Be sure, dear friend, that your place in my heart is ever reserved and warm! I wish, when I recovered, I could come to see you. But I am afraid this is not possible. Your dear father had gone to Port Said for a time when I left Haifa. The Master is in splendid health. Fourteen American pilgrims have arrived. The Holy Land is astir![143]

On Monday, 17 May 1920 Shoghi Effendi wrote to Ali Kuli Khan from Neuilly. In this letter he expressed his disappointment at having missed the unannounced visit of Ali Kuli Khan and his family during the weekend. Shoghi Effendi said he wished that Ali Kuli Khan would inform him of his intended visits so that he might postpone his stroll to receive him. During the previous few days, he said, he had not been feeling well and his appetite had completely faded. The physician intended to prescribe him some medicine and keep him in bed for one whole day. Shoghi Effendi commented that it had been a long time since a spiritual breeze had wafted from the Holy Land and the absence of news had affected his health and caused him sorrow. He hoped that soon a sign would appear from 'Abdu'l-Bahá which would breathe a new life into him. At the conclusion of the letter, Shoghi Effendi states his intention to visit Ali Kuli Khan before the end of the week.[144]

Soon after this Shoghi Effendi felt well enough to visit the friends. He accepted an invitation to dinner at the home of Ali Kuli Khan although Khan himself was away. On the day of his visit Shoghi Effendi wrote to him saying how much he was missed and assuring him of his prayers. In this letter Shoghi Effendi reported on his progress, stating that his physical health was improving although he was still undergoing treatment. He repeated that he has not received any news from the Holy Land and was therefore overcome with considerable sorrow, which aggravated his ill health. He asked Ali Kuli Khan to please inform him of any news he may receive from the Master, as such news was the balm to the heart of one who is away from the land of his Beloved.[145]

Application to Oxford

Having translated so many Tablets of the Master, Shoghi Effendi was aware of the challenge presented by the task of translation. He did not feel that his rendering of the Master's Tablets in English conveyed the charm and beauty of the originals. Furthermore, he had read the translations of the sacred writings of Bahá'u'lláh by other believers and was not happy with them. Translation of the holy words required someone with proficiency in three languages: Arabic, Persian and English. To communicate the beauty of the creative words in his English translations, Shoghi Effendi needed to perfect his command of the English language. Several of the English friends and admirers of the Master had recommended Oxford University as the environment where he might pursue this goal. The Master also wished that Shoghi Effendi receive further education in England, although a definite decision had not been made.

On Friday, 11 June 1920 Shoghi Effendi sent a letter of application from Neuilly to Oxford University seeking admission to that great centre of learning and describing clearly his intended course of study:

Dear Sir:–

My esteemed friend Sir Herbert Samuel advises me to write you inquiring about admission as a non-collegiate student at Balliol College or any other college at Oxford University. My sole aim is to perfect my English, to acquire the literary ability to write it well, speak it well & translate correctly & eloquently from Persian & Arabic into English. My aim is to concentrate for two years upon this object & to acquire it through the help of a tutor, by attending lectures, by associating with cultured & refined literary circles & by receiving exercises in Phonetics. I would be much obliged if you could help me along that line.

Yours very sincerely,
Shoghi Rabbani[146]

On Thursday, 24 June 1920 Shoghi Effendi wrote to Mr Scott, a devoted believer residing in Paris. By this time

Shoghi Effendi's health had improved enough to enable him to participate in Bahá'í activities.

> My dear brother!
>
> Your letter has been read with great joy but how much I miss you & we miss you all! Our meetings are expanding, gaining in spirit & becoming more & more elaborate. We had a splendid meeting last Tuesday at Akbar's – Mirza Gholam Ali had returned from Berlin & Dr Mirza had come from Mesopotamia & India. Some twenty were present at the meeting, including the Dreyfuses & Lotfullah.
>
> As to my health, I have <u>fully</u> recovered but deplore the fact that no news reaches me from home. Ever since your departure I have received no letter & no cable except a letter from Edith Sanderson from Vevey. I am afraid the post is not properly forwarding my letters. I have been to the concierge & no letters. I shall go again to-day. I hope something will put an end to my eager anticipation. I shall send you the photographs we took of the Holy Sites in Paris as soon as they are ready. Meanwhile I hope you will send me the picture we took together at your home. Oh! your lovely blessed abode! What a cluster of sweet memories & associations cling around it! I shall never forget our last interview under its roof.[147]

On Monday, 28 June 1920 Shoghi Effendi wrote to Ali Yazdi from Neuilly responding to a letter he had received from his friend:

> My dear unforgettable 'Alí!
>
> Your letter and the good news of you imparted by Ghulám-'Alí made me wish or yearn to come to you and see you for a few days now that I am better and almost fully recovered! I shall wait and see the turn of events b fore I decide to pass a sojourn with you in Berlin. Now that I have recovered . . . I am impatient to plunge again in a valuable, profitable work, to build the structure for my future and

whether I shall resume my work in Haifa or go to England for two years study – it all depends upon the Master's will, which shall be communicated to me within a fortnight.

I have deplored the hard financial situation you are in, and I really feel with you. I have just written home and exposed your situation to the Holy Mother, and I trust something will be done to remedy the situation. Dr Mírzá has lately arrived here from Baghdad . . . Who knows? Perhaps we may both come and see you for some days in Berlin! It is a long time I have received no news from home, and I am growing impatient . . . President Bliss has died in America. A great blow indeed to the college! I do not like Paris. People are so superficial, empty, pleasure-seeking, and frivolous. Life bores me here, and I hope I will have soon a change for the better.

Your loving brother
Shoghi[148]

The reference made in this letter to Ali Yazdi's financial condition shows the compassion of Shoghi Effendi for a friend in need. Ali Yazdi had left the Holy Land hoping to earn his living as a draftsman. However, owing to the economic condition of post-war Germany with its high inflation and scarcity of jobs, he found it difficult to manage financially and save money for his college course, which the Master had instructed him to pursue. His only reserve was the one hundred English pounds that 'Abdu'l-Bahá had given him.[149]

On Friday, 2 July 1920 Dr Esslemont received a letter from Shoghi Effendi stating that he was awaiting the Master's decision about whether he should return to Haifa or go to England.[150]

Mrs Sheybání, one of the believers residing in Paris, had invited Shoghi Effendi to visit Versailles. Shoghi Effendi accepted her invitation and planned the visit for Sunday, 4 July 1920. On this day, Shoghi Effendi was setting out on his trip when he received a telephone message from Mme

Dreyfus that at last a message has been received from the Holy Land that everyone was well. This joyous news was what Shoghi Effendi had been waiting for. It made him so happy that all the events of that day were pleasing to him. It was a perfect beginning to a perfect day.[151]

When he returned from Versailles another blessing awaited him. Shoghi Effendi describes his joy on this day in a letter to Mrs Sheybání written on Monday, 5 July 1920 from Neuilly:

My dear & affectionate Baha'i sister:

A thousand thanks for your invitation to Versailles which has proved to be pregnant with many good results. Would such an invitation on your part necessarily entail such pleasing consequences & usher in such a brilliant morn of joy, satisfaction & assurance, I undoubtedly would have sought it every day from you for you can't imagine with what refreshing news yesterday's trip to Versailles opened & with what an event it ended. The whole day has been a remarkable one, as I & my friend have reiterated it over and over again to Mr Sheybany, who did a great deal to please & satisfy us – what a great impression the 'grandes eaux' . . . made upon me and to what magnificent, sumptuous & historically remarkable apartments we were led! Our lunch was even unexpectedly delightful & most palatable. I do not think that the big concourse of people around us had such a fine lunch. The day in spite of its sombre look in the morning was a perfect one. In the midst of the gloom and the dreariness of the morning, just at the moment I was stepping out to meet Sheybani, I got a telephone message from Mme Dreyfus that at last a message has been received from the Holy Land to the effect that all are well! What a happy beginning to a splendid day! When I returned, another blessing & joy awaited me as if to crown this great day:– letters for me directly from Haifa which had been only 10 days en route with a note from the post informing me of a registered letter in my name! Oh! how my joy would be complete & how it would overflow! I mention these simply to tell you that in the coming days & years this first visit to Versailles will be closely associated with such delightful experiences & lively recollections . . .[152]

The communication Shoghi Effendi received from the Holy Land helped him to make his decision about his future. The Master had not only wished him to continue his education in England but had also given him instructions on how to pursue admission into Oxford University. Despite the great love the Master had for Shoghi Effendi and His desire to be with him during the last years of His life on this physical plane, He knew the great destiny of His beloved grandson and wished him to continue his preparation for his destined mission.

Shoghi Effendi's education at Oxford was not only an important stage in his life but also a stage in the unfoldment of a Divine Plan for humankind. The Master had communicated His intention to send His grandson to England while Shoghi Effendi was still in high school. Rúḥíyyih Khánum records the recollections of a German woman physician, Dr J. Fallscheer, some eleven years after her visit to attend the ladies of 'Abdu'l-Bahá's household. Dr Fallscheer's account indicates the Master's desire to send Shoghi Effendi to Oxford:

At this moment the son-in-law [the husband of the eldest daughter of 'Abdu'l-Bahá] entered the room . . . At first I did not notice that behind the tall, dignified man his eldest son, Shoghi Effendi, had entered the room and greeted his venerable grandfather . . . I had already seen the child fleetingly on a few other occasions . . . I never removed my eyes from the still very youthful grandson of Abbas Effendi . . . The boy remained motionless in his place and submissive in his attitude. After his father and the man with him had taken their leave of the Master, his father whispered

65

something to him as he went out, whereupon the youth, in a slow and measured manner, like a grown up person, approached his beloved grandfather, waited to be addressed, answered distinctly in Persian and was laughingly dismissed . . .

Abbas Effendi rose and came over to us . . . 'Now my daughter,' He began, 'How do you like my future Elisha?' 'Master, if I may speak openly, I must say that in his boy's face are the dark eyes of a sufferer, one who will suffer a great deal!' Thoughtfully the Master looked beyond us into space and after a long time turned His gaze back to us and said: 'My grandson does not have the eyes of a trailblazer, a fighter or a victor, but in his eyes one sees deep loyalty, perseverance and conscientiousness. And do you know why, my daughter, he will fall heir to the heavy inheritance of being my Vazir?' Without waiting for my reply, looking more at His dear sister than at me, as if He had forgotten my presence, He went on: 'Bahá'u'lláh, the Great Perfection – blessed be His words – in the past, the present and forever – chose this insignificant one to be His successor, not because I was the first born, but because His inner eye had already discerned on my brow the seal of God.

'Before His ascension into eternal Light the blessed Manifestation reminded me that I too – irrespective of primogeniture or age – must observe among my sons and grandsons whom God would indicate for His office. My sons passed to eternity in their tenderest years, in my line, among my relatives, only little Shoghi has the shadow of a great calling in the depths of his eyes.' There followed another long pause, then the Master turned again to me and said: 'At the present time the British Empire is the greatest and is still expanding and its language is a world language. My future Vazir shall receive the preparation for his weighty office in England itself, after he has obtained here in Palestine a fundamental knowledge of the oriental languages and the wisdom of the East.' Whereupon I ventured to interject: 'Will not the western education, the English training, remould his nature, confine his versatile mind in the rigid bonds of intellectualism, stifle through dogma and convention his oriental irrationality and intuition so that he will no longer be a servant of the Almighty but rather a slave to the rationality of western opportunism and the shallowness of every day life?' Long pause! Then Abbas Effendi 'Abdu'l-Bahá rose and in a strong and solemn voice said: 'I am not giving my Elisha to the British to educate. I dedicate and give him to the Almighty. God's eyes watch over my child in Oxford as well – Inshallah!'[153]

Thus, the hand of destiny propelled Shoghi Effendi to turn his attention to England. Unaware that his sojourn in that country would keep him separated from his beloved grandfather and would prevent him from ever again attaining His presence on this physical plane, Shoghi Effendi proceeded to London in conformity with the will of 'Abdu'l-Bahá. His departure from Paris took place within two weeks of receiving the Master's communication.

8

Arrival in England

Shoghi Effendi arrived in the United Kingdom in mid-July 1920 and was welcomed by a community of devoted believers and admirers of the Faith who had been nurtured by their loving Master. Prominent among the believers and admirers of the Master were Lady Blomfield, Major Tudor-Pole and Lord Lamington.

Lady Blomfield, one of the pillars of the Cause in England, had been among the first to recognize the new revelation. She was a woman whose considerable influence traced back to her father-in-law, Dr Charles James Blomfield (1786–1857), the Bishop of London and the tutor of Queen Victoria. Lady Blomfield and her daughter Mary had been introduced to the Faith at a reception in Paris in 1907. Their teacher was Miss Bertha Herbert. Both had embraced the Faith upon their return to England and were nurtured by a Bahá'í community comprising two people: an American believer living in London, Mrs Thornburgh-Cropper, and Miss Ethel Rosenberg, the first British woman to accept the new Faith of God.

Lord Lamington, one-time Governor of the Bombay Presidency, was another admirer of 'Abdu'l-Bahá living in London in 1920. On Christmas day 1912 the Master had visited Lord Lamington in London. During that visit Lord Lamington had been deeply touched by the message of peace and goodwill that flowed through the words and example of the Master. When he discovered in the spring of 1918 from Lady Blomfield that 'Abdu'l-Bahá was in danger in the Holy

Land, he dispatched a letter to the Foreign Office explaining the danger facing the Master and the importance of His work for peace. Exerting his influence, he made sure that the letter was put into the hands of Lord Balfour, Secretary of State for Foreign Affairs. It was this intervention that produced the instruction to General Allenby to extend every protection necessary to 'Abdu'l-Bahá. Later, in 1919, when Lamington was directing the Syrian Relief work from his headquarters in Damascus, he called on 'Abdu'l-Bahá to receive His blessings and visited Him again to bid farewell. It was on this occasion that he received the ring of the Master.[154]

When Shoghi Effendi arrived in England he was carrying with him Tablets from the Master to Lady Blomfield, Lord Lamington and Major Tudor-Pole which expressed the Master's wish for the education of His grandson. During the one week Shoghi Effendi stayed in London, he delivered the Master's Tablets to these individuals and secured introductions to eminent professors and orientalists at Oxford and London Universities, including Sir Denison Ross and Professor Ker.[155]

Sir Denison Ross, the Director of Oriental Studies at the London School of Oriental Studies since 1916, was an eminent scholar who had studied oriental languages in Paris and Strasburg and had held the position of Professor of Persian at University College, London.[156]

Professor William Ker was Professor of English Literature at University College, London. He later became Fellow of All Souls College, Oxford.[157]

Visit with the Bahá'ís in London

The Bahá'í community of London had grown considerably since its inception in 1899. The Master's first visit to Britain in 1911, lasting one month, nurtured this community and prepared it for its great destiny in the service of the Cause.

London and Bristol were the two cities blessed by His presence during this first visit. It was in London that He addressed large gatherings of people of the West for the first time. He stayed as the guest of Lady Blomfield in London for the entire period, except for three days in Bristol.[158]

By the time the Master visited Britain for the second time, the community had grown. Receptions and large public gatherings were organized for Him in several cities including, Liverpool and Edinburgh.

After this second visit the activities had multiplied everywhere in England. At the end of the war the Bahá'ís of London began to hold regular meetings at Lindsay Hall in Notting Hill Gate.[159]

Upon his arrival in England in 1920, Shoghi Effendi visited the believers in Lindsay Hall. On Wednesday, 21 July Dr Esslemont met Shoghi Effendi there and later described this visit in a letter to Dr Luṭfu'lláh Ḥakím:

> I was delighted to see him and we embraced in true oriental fashion. Then shortly Mr and Mrs Ober turned up too, so we had a real Bahai meeting with both East and West well represented. I spoke shortly, then both of the Obers, and then Shoghi spoke and chanted. Miss Rosenberg was in the chair and seemed very happy. The hall was full and all seemed to enjoy the meeting greatly.[160]

The next day Dr Esslemont called on Shoghi Effendi at his hotel and went with him to Miss Grand's home where the Obers were staying. On Friday, 23 July Dr Esslemont met Shoghi Effendi again after lunch at Miss Rosenberg's. Together they went to Miss Grand's home that evening where 17 people, many of whom had never heard of the Cause before, were present.

Miss Herrick had hoped a unity meeting could be arranged while Shoghi Effendi was in London. She had felt the need for some organization and cooperation among the

friends and had tried hard to arrange such a meeting, but
found it impossible and was much disappointed. On Saturday
morning Dr Esslemont came to London to meet Shoghi
Effendi, and as he had no prior engagement, they both went
to see Miss Herrick. Esslemont states:

> We had a fine talk together, and she became much happier.
> When it came near lunch-time I proposed that she should
> come and lunch with us somewhere, but we were sitting in
> the garden where it was nice and sunny. So Shoghi sug-
> gested that it would be much nicer to have a picnic lunch,
> so the three of us sallied forth with a basket to buy some
> fruit and things for lunch, and we had a jolly little lunch in
> the garden. We decided that Miss Herrick should see Miss
> Rosenberg and some of the others to try to arrange a Unity
> meeting for Tuesday. The Obers and I both had to leave
> London yesterday, but Shoghi hoped to attend the meetings
> on both Tuesday and Wednesday next. Shoghi suggested
> that a meeting of the Council of the London Group should
> be held at a time when as many of the members as possible
> could attend, when some more definite arrangements could
> be agreed upon with regard to the holding of feasts for the
> year, and a committee appointed to see to the details.[161]

After meeting the Bahá'ís in London, Shoghi Effendi's next
destination was Oxford. He wished to follow up on the letter
of application to Oxford University, which he had sent to
Balliol College from Paris.

City of Oxford

The city of Oxford, once a walled medieval city and the scene
of significant events in British history, including its selection
by Charles I as his headquarters (1642–6) during the Civil
War, had become recognized by the 18th century as one of
Europe's great intellectual centres.

71

Balliol College[162]

Balliol, one of the two oldest colleges in Oxford, is part of a unique English collegiate system with origins in 12th century France. Hotel Dieu in Paris, established through the endowment of an English pilgrim in 1180, was initially an experiment. It was later imitated and improved upon in France and gradually evolved into the collegiate system in England.[163] In the 13th century, Oxford colleges were founded after the French models by individual benefactors.

The founding of Balliol emerged from a dispute between the secular and ecclesiastical powers over the rights to the possession of lands. The Balliols of Barnard Castle were among the highest ranking of the northern nobility. John Balliol, the head of the house of Balliol, vastly expanded his properties through his marriage to Lady Dervorguilla. He ruled over his vast estate as a petty sovereign. Yet, despite his powers, he faced bitter conflicts directed by the Bishop of Durham, Walter Kirkham.

The story of Balliol College begins in the year 1255 when the bishop excommunicated some of the Balliol retainers over disputed lands. Balliol laid an ambush for the bishop and subjected him to various indignities. The bishop put his complaint before the king and obtained a writ condemning Balliol and demanding instant reparation.

Balliol lost some of his possessions as a result of this dispute. He was forced by the bishop to crown the settlement with a substantial act of charity. In obedience to the mandate, John Balliol hired a house in the suburbs of Oxford and made it a hostel for the reception of 16 poor scholars, to whom he gave an allowance of eight pence a day. This house, located in Horsemonger Street, which is today's Broad Street, became known as Old Balliol Hall or Sparrow Hall.

The credit for completing what John Balliol had begun belongs to his wife, Lady Dervorguilla of Galloway, who after her husband's death continued to be the champion of his hostel until her own death in the year 1289. She spent her money and her energies serving the scholars of Balliol.

The Old Balliol Hall survived the ecclesiastical disputes of the next seven centuries. In mid-16th century the College, a staunch supporter of Rome, tried to resist Henry VIII's demand that his supremacy be acknowledged and escaped the king's wrath. Later, on the accession of Mary in 1553, James Brookes, the Master of Balliol, was appointed Bishop of Gloucester and became one of the judges who condemned the Protestant Bishops Latimer, Ridley and Cranmer to be burned in Broad Street.[164] The Martyrs' memorial, which Shoghi Effendi is reported to have viewed from his room in college,[165] was erected in 1843 near the back gate of the college close to the spot outside the Master's lodging where the bishops perished.

By 1920 Balliol College had become one of the finest centres of learning in the world. The number of students studying there had increased over the years from the original 16 to more than a hundred in the 18th century and about two hundred in 1920. The numbers enrolled had picked up after a sharp decrease during the World War.[166]

During Shoghi Effendi's stay at Balliol, two keys personages at the college were A. L. Smith and A. D. Lindsay.

A. L. Smith

Smith, the Master of Balliol in 1920, had succeeded J. L. Strachan in 1916 at the age of 66. He was known among the students for his ability to draw attention to some aspect or interpretation of facts that had not occurred to them.[167]

Smith showed great interest in the people he met. He was keen to hear about their lives, activities and problems, and was always interested in helping them.[168]

A. D. Lindsay

Alexander Dunlop Lindsay was Fellow and classical tutor of the college from 1906. He was one of the chief pioneers in the establishment of Modern Greats. In 1907 he published a translation of Plato's *Republic*. He was one of the promoters of the course 'Philosophy, Politics and Economics' at Oxford. He later introduced the Science Greats, combining philosophy with the principles of natural science, for which he had failed to win acceptance.[169]

Lindsay had the reputation of being an outstanding tutor who had an exceptional human sympathy and was ready to help an undergraduate student needing his support. He had clear views of his own; however, he was open to fresh ideas. He believed that it was the business of the college to make the students find out what their own views were and to impress upon them their duty to think seriously and with knowledge. Lindsay influenced the students without attempting to convert them to his opinions. His aim was to raise the discussion of a problem to a higher level.[170]

Arrival in Oxford

The city of Oxford had been blessed by the footsteps of the Master and was about to receive His grandson, Shoghi Effendi, who arrived during the week of 26 July 1920. He stayed at the Randolph Hotel. He had already met Sir Denison Ross and Professor William Ker, from whom he had received introductions to Professor Margoliouth and Sir Walter Raleigh.

Sir Walter Raleigh had been Professor of English at Liverpool and Glasgow before his appointment in 1904 as the first Professor of English Literature at the University of Oxford. He was a Fellow of Merton College.[171]

74

Professor Margoliouth was an Arabic scholar and orientalist who had been the Laudian Professor of Arabic in Oxford since 1889 and became Fellow of the British Academy in 1915. During the years 1919–22, he was Professor of Arabic at New College. He had the reputation of being a great Arabic scholar and lectured in Arabic in Cairo during the War.[172]

It was through these professors, and particularly Sir Walter Raleigh, that Shoghi Effendi was introduced to the Master of Balliol College, A. L. Smith. In a letter Shoghi Effendi wrote from the Randolph Hotel on Wednesday, 28 July 1920 to Mrs Ali Kuli Khan in Paris, he states:

> . . . before leaving for Oxford, I had a letter from Margoliouth saying that he would do all in his power to be of help to a relative of 'Abdu'l-Bahá. With this man and the Master of Balliol College – a College from which great men such as Lord Grey, Earl Curzon, Lord Milner, Mr Asquith, Swinburne and Sir Herbert Samuel have graduated – I had the opportunity of speaking about the Cause and clearing up some points that to these busy scholars had hitherto been uncertain and confused.
>
> Do pray for me, as I have requested you on the eve of my departure, that in this great intellectual centre I may attain my object and achieve my end . . .[173]

A few days later, on 8 August 1920, Lord Lamington wrote to 'Abdu'l-Bahá describing his visit with Shoghi Effendi and telling the Master that he was again impressed by Shoghi Effendi's 'intelligence and open honest manner'. He said that Shoghi Effendi had visited the House of Lords two or three times.[174]

On the same day, 8 August, Shoghi Effendi wrote a postcard to Luṭfu'lláh Ḥakím in Haifa reporting his progress in the previous two weeks and indicating that he had found a tutor, a professor of philosophy:

... I have settled at Oxford, have taken hold of a tutor who is professor of philosophy at Balliol ... Lady Blomfield, Mrs Cropper, Miss Rosenberg, Lord Lamington, Tudor Pole and particularly Mrs Whyte have been of great help. I met Dr Esslemont and Miss Herrick and have addressed the meeting at Lindsay Hall. I have promised to address another meeting at Miss Herrick's, but presently I am absorbed in arranging for my immediate studies and my entering for the academic year. I am keeping well and fresh. I feel rather lonely but the immense Bodleian library, the different summer schools at the various colleges ... keep me busy.

Shoghi[175]

Mrs Whyte, an admirer of 'Abdu'l-Bahá, was the wife of Dr Alexander Whyte, an eminent member of the Free Church of Scotland. She had visited 'Akká in 1906 and had written an account of her visit, which appears in volume 4 of *The Bahá'í World*. While in 'Akká she had seen the young Shoghi Effendi and had been moved when she observed the devotion and reverence of the child in the Shrine of Bahá'u'lláh. She had wondered then what destiny lay before this boy of tender years.[176] That memory was vivid in her mind when she and her husband welcomed Shoghi Effendi to their home in 1920.

The academic term would not start until October. Many students were in Oxford visiting the university before the term to arrange their accommodation and then return home for the remainder of the long vacation. Shoghi Effendi, however, could not wait for the term to begin. He was anxious to get started and did not wish to waste any time. He immediately commenced his work with the assistance of a tutor. He spent his time both with this tutor and in the Bodleian Library.

On Friday, 10 September, having already spent a few concentrated weeks of study in Oxford, Shoghi Effendi accepted the invitation of Dr Esslemont to visit him in Bournemouth for a few days and stay in the sanatorium where Dr Esslemont practised. Shoghi Effendi's sister Rúḥangíz joined him the next day. A Persian believer, Aflátún, joined this group.

Dr Esslemont refers to Shoghi Effendi's visit in a letter he wrote to Dr Luṭfu'lláh Ḥakím at the conclusion of the visit, on Wednesday, 15 September, the day Shoghi Effendi left Bournemouth to return to Oxford:

> Shoghi Effendi is very well. He seems to be in better health and spirits than when I was at Haifa . . . Shoghi Effendi seems to be very keen on his studies and to be making very satisfactory progress.[177]

Upon his return to Oxford Shoghi Effendi answered the correspondence he had received and on Friday, 17 September 1920 he wrote a letter to Mr and Mrs Scott in Paris:

My dear Bahai brother & sister:

I have received your kind & affectionate letter enclosing the photographs you have so kindly sent me. I have been so busy & am still so absorbed in my studies that I have scarcely found any time to have my films developed but I shall send you the pictures I took at Operville as soon as they are ready.

I have been immersed in my studies – all having as an end a better ability in translating the words of Baha'u'llah and a fuller knowledge & better expression in expounding its principles.

I have come, in the course of my readings at the University Bodleian library, across some rare & authoritative books, written by eminent statesmen & touching the Bahai Movement. Among them is Earl Curzon's [Secretary of State for Foreign Affairs] book on Persia written in 1892 wherein he writes the following: 'The lowest estimate places them (the Babis) in Persia at half a million. I am disposed to think that the total (in Persia) is nearer one million . . . Tales of magnificent heroism illumine the blood-stained pages of Babi

77

history. Ignorant & unlettered as many of its votaries are & have been, they are yet prepared to die for their religion & the fires of Smithfield did not kindle a nobler courage than has met & defied the more-refined torture-mongers of Tihran. Of no small account, then, must be the tenets of a creed that can awaken in its followers so rare & beautiful a spirit of self-sacrifice . . . Beauty & the female sex also lent their consecration to the new creed & the heroism of the lovely but ill-fated poetess of Kazvin, Kurrotu'l-ayn, who throwing off the veil, carried the missionary torch far & wide, is one of the most affecting episodes in modern history . . .' This is a sample of the work I am plunging in & I always seek your prayers that I may one day, fully-equipped, render a distinguished service to the threshold of Baha'u'llah.

Yours very affectionately,

Shoghi[178]

Shoghi Effendi with Dr John Esslemont in Bournemouth, England

University of Oxford.
SCHOLARES NON ASCRIPTI.

Mr. Shawqi Rabbani _____ entered by Matriculation as a Non-Collegiate Student 23 October 1920 and has kept by residence one _____ Terms

Michaelmas _____ 1920

_____ 19__

_____ 19__

_____ 19__

His name has been on the Books of the Students' Delegacy for one _____ Terms. He is of good character and has the permission of the Delegates to migrate to Balliol College

16 Jany. 1921

J. Bernard Baker
Censor.

No. 14

Shoghi Effendi's Certificate of Matriculation

Shoghi Effendi during his stay in England

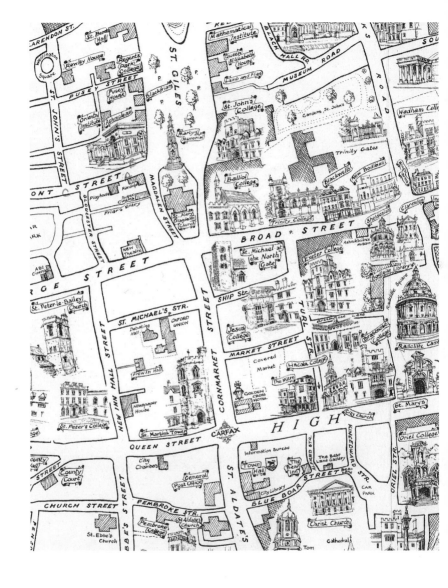

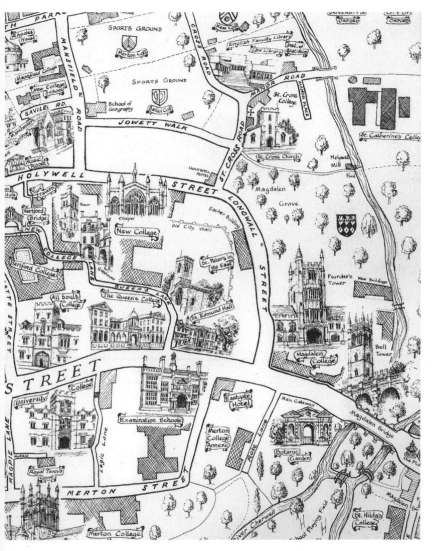

Blackwells Map of Oxford (1966) Drawn by Brian Cairns

Non-Collegiate Delegacy.

To be filled up and transmitted to the Office
by the end of the first week of Term.

Michalmas Term, 192

Name *Sh. Rabbani*

Course proposed *Economics & Social Sciences*

Lectures

Master of Balliol : Soc. + Pol. Questions
Rev. Carlyle   Soc. + Ind. Questions
Penson   Elem. Economics
Carlyle   Pol. Science

Tutor *Mr. Lindsey*

Shoghi Effendi's course proposal

29

University of Oxford.
Certificate of Migration.

—

The Proctors have seen the testimonial

of Mr. S. Rahbani _____ and his permission to

migrate from _Mon Coll_ _____ and

know of no reason why he should not be allowed to migrate to

Ball: Coll. _____

_____

G.B. Allen } Proctors.

Y₂ j. f̄ Tₘ

Date _____ Jan 17. 1921

Certificate of Migration

Letter written by Shoghi Effendi from Balliol College, 28 January 1921

9

Matriculation at Oxford

Sir Walter Raleigh's introduction was instrumental in the warm reception accorded to Shoghi Effendi by the Master of Balliol College, A. L. Smith. Through Smith, Shoghi Effendi was introduced to a Fellow of Balliol College, A. D. Lindsay, who held the position of classical tutor and Jowett Lecturer in Philosophy. Lindsay was very impressed with Shoghi Effendi and accepted to be his tutor. However, with the college admissions already announced, he felt he could not immediately admit Shoghi Effendi to Balliol.

Lindsay was aware that there might be a vacancy in Balliol because it was possible a Japanese student was not going to turn up. However, he did not disclose this fact to Shoghi Effendi. He wanted to be sure that the Japanese student was not coming and he wanted to be sure the college would officially accept Shoghi Effendi. He felt Shoghi Effendi should wait until the first college meeting after the completion of the first term, when admissions were considered. This would be the Monday after the beginning of the term.

Lindsay decided, early in October, that rather than admit Shoghi Effendi to Balliol, he would have him registered in a non-college institution affiliated with Oxford University known as the Non-Collegiate Delegacy.[179]

Background on the Non-Collegiate Delegacy

In the year 1868 young men were permitted under certain conditions to become students and members of Oxford

79

University without being members of a College or Hall. Such persons kept their residence in houses or licensed lodgings within the limit of a circle a mile and a half in radius from Carfax.[180] These students enjoyed the same privileges available to other students.

The admission of students into the University and the supervision of their work during their residence in Oxford were the responsibility of a Delegacy consisting of a Vice Chancellor, Proctors, a Censor, a Controller of Lodging Houses and six Members of Convocation holding office for six years. The Censor, nominated by the Vice Chancellor and Proctors,[181] supervised the students and was charged with the care of their conduct and studies. The Censor of the Non-Collegiate Delegacy in 1920 was James Bernard Baker.

The Non-Collegiate Delegacy adopted the name St Catherine's Society in 1930 and occupied permanent buildings in 1936. Members of the Society were required to keep their statutable residence in Oxford in houses approved by the Delegacy of Lodgings. They were considered members of the University and enjoyed the same privileges as other students. In 1962 St Catherine's Society received college status and became known as St Catherine's College.[182]

Shoghi Effendi in the Non-Collegiate Delegacy

On 7 October 1920 Lindsay wrote to J. B. Baker introducing Shoghi Effendi. As Censor, Baker would be required to look after Shoghi Effendi and be his tutor.

Expressing his very high opinion of Shoghi Effendi, Lindsay suggested that Baker should matriculate Shoghi Effendi in the Non-Collegiate Delegacy. He indicated that if Baker had difficulty in giving tuition to Shoghi Effendi, he himself would 'look after him in the meantime'. Lindsay ended his letter by saying, 'He is a quite exceptional young man.'[183]

In his letter to Baker, Lindsay mentioned that at one time he had hoped there would be a vacancy in Balliol that could be filled by Shoghi Effendi but that 'the prospect was not fulfilled'. Later correspondence shows that the Japanese student never came and that Shoghi Effendi could have been admitted to begin his work in Balliol during the first term.

Lindsay's decision meant that Shoghi Effendi would not be able to move to Balliol or 'migrate into college' during the first term. Postponing the decision to the 'Monday after full term' meant that Shoghi Effendi would not be able to move into Balliol in the second term either, inasmuch as according to the rules, notice for migration or movement into college must be given in the sixth week of the previous term.[184]

This caused tremendous inconvenience and disappointment for Shoghi Effendi, who was confident Balliol was where he was meant to study. He 'had made up his mind' he would be admitted and had been counting on moving into Balliol during the first term. Shoghi Effendi was not pleased with the prospect of having to matriculate in the Non-Collegiate Delegacy. He was keen to settle into his room in the college and concentrate his energies on his work.

In a letter to Ali Yazdi dated Sunday, 10 October 1920 Shoghi Effendi shares his painful disappointments and anxieties regarding his entrance into Balliol College:

Dear 'Alí:

Your letter reached me at a time I was immersed heart and soul in my manifold preparations for entrance at Balliol College, Oxford. I am fearfully anxious and occupied, but your letter absorbed my interest and diverted it from this phase for a time. I am glad and extremely sad in receiving your letter – glad at the knowledge that at last my efforts have proved partially successful and *some* pecuniary help has been extended to you.[185] I wished, dear 'Alí, to have had enough money at my disposal to share it with you! I immediately wrote to Mrs George and exposed the case fully. I hope

81

you will soon and easily sail. I am so grieved at the sudden turn of events and the complications and cost of travel have only marred the brightness caused by the knowledge that some financial help has been finally extended . . .

I assure you, dear friend, that if some are free from pecuniary anxieties, they are nevertheless subject to another set of various physical, intellectual, and social drawbacks and preoccupations. Do you believe me when I say that I, the grandson of the Master, have been victim of painful experiences, sometimes of bitter disappointments, and always of constant anxieties – all justified – for my immediate work and future? If you have spent of late painful and trying times, my share of these troubled hours is by no means much less and my burden much lighter.

My field of study is so *vast*, I have to acquire, master, and digest so many facts, courses, and books – all essential, all indispensable to my future career in the Cause. The very extent of this immense field is enough to discourage, excite, and overwhelm such a young and inexperienced beginner as myself. Think of the vast field of Economics; of social conditions and problems; of the various religions of the past, their histories and their principles and their force; the acquisition of a sound and literary ability in English to be served for translation purposes; the mastery of public speaking so essential to me, all these and a dozen more – all to be sought, acquired, and digested!

Prayer, faith, perseverance and effort will alone do it. Praying for your success from all my heart!

Shoghi Rabbani[186]

10

Student Life at Oxford

Although Shoghi Effendi did not register in Balliol during the first term, he was in the college every day and received tuition from A. D. Lindsay. He looked forward to moving into the college living quarters from his outside lodgings. The student living quarters surround Balliol Hall. They had been constructed over seven centuries before the student days of Shoghi Effendi. These buildings include, additionally, a Junior Common Room (JCR), a chapel, a library and a dining hall. Students live in buildings surrounding the administrative quarters of the college.[187]

Most members of the college live in college buildings known as staircases. Others live in housing outside the college. The student quarters in college are mostly large and spacious and often include separate areas for a bedroom and a living room. Access to the living quarters is not by corridors but by staircases, each of which leads to two or more quarters on each of its floors.[188]

The college non-academic staff consists of the porter, the kitchen staff and the scouts. The scouts are responsible for looking after the comfort of students. They wake up the students in the mornings, clean their rooms and serve them meals in the dining hall.

Gowns

When Shoghi Effendi attended Oxford the students were required to wear appropriate gowns most of the time. The Scholars wore floor-length black flowing gowns, the Exhibitioners and Commoners wore shorter gowns and those students pursuing post-graduate courses wore gowns extending to mid-calf. Shoghi Effendi, being a graduate student, probably wore a gown of the latter type.[189]

Meals and Daily Routine

Most students follow a traditional basic daily routine. They are awakened every morning by their scouts. They are then served breakfast in the hall. Breakfast consists of fruit juice, eggs, bacon, sausage or fish, toast and honey or marmalade. After breakfast, students usually retire to the JCR to read the morning papers before attending their respective lectures.

Lunch is usually served in the hall between one and two o'clock in the afternoon. After lunch the students meet their tutors or work in the library on assignments given by their tutors. Around 3:30 p.m. many students return to the JCR to have tea, often with their guests, to write letters or to read the papers. Dinner is served in the hall around 6 to 7:30 p.m.

After dinner students return to the JCR for coffee and discussion. A few spend time in the library, study in their quarters or visit each other in their rooms. The evenings are spent studying, attending meetings, going to the Student Union debates and so on. At the time of Shoghi Effendi the students were expected to be back in the college by nine in the evening or pay a gate fine.[190]

While this leisurely schedule was practised more or less by the majority of the students, Shoghi Effendi did not have time to waste. He took advantage of every minute to pursue the learning objective he had set for himself or to translate the writings into English.

Academic Work

Academic work is supervised by tutors who help students choose their subjects and arrange for their lectures. The students are encouraged to attend lectures offered by Oxford

84

University often held in the departmental buildings or inside the colleges.

In addition to the lectures, students are required to meet with their tutors for specific work. Tutors assign particular topics to the students for study and give them roughly a week to research the topic and write an appropriate essay. The students are expected to consult numerous sources in the college library and in the university Bodleian library. When the essay is completed, the students must read the essay in the presence of their tutor and other students and receive the tutor's criticism. This exercise helps prepare them for the university's final examination.[191]

The prestige and reputation of each college depends on how well its students perform academically in the university final examinations and later in life.

Academic Year

The academic year is divided into three terms of approximately eight weeks separated by vacation periods. The first term, the Michaelmas Term, begins early in October and ends in December before Christmas. The second term, the Hilary Term, begins in January and ends in late March. The third term, Trinity Term, begins in April and ends late in June. The Trinity term is followed by a long vacation.[192]

11

Michaelmas Term 1920

The Michaelmas term was already beginning when Lindsay wrote his first letter to Baker about Shoghi Effendi. The lectures were due to start a few days later. Yet Shoghi Effendi's registration status was not clear in early October. Nevertheless, Shoghi Effendi attended lectures and continued his work.

Shoghi Effendi's notebook shows a list of lectures he was planning to attend during the week of 11–16 October 1920:[193]

Monday	Logic – Mr Ross M.A.
Tuesday	Political Economy – Sir T. H. Penson M.A. Eastern Questions – F. F. Urquhart M.A.
Wednesday	Social and Industrial Questions – Rev. Carlyle
Thursday	Political Science – Rev. Carlyle
Friday	Social and Political Problems – Mr Smith (Master of Balliol)
Saturday	English Economic History since 1668 – Sir T. H. Penson M.A.

Despite the pressure of work and the frustration he felt related to his admission into Balliol College, Shoghi Effendi found time for service to the Cause. Dr Esslemont had sent his book to Shoghi Effendi. On 13 October 1920 Dr Esslemont wrote to Dr Luṭfu'lláh Ḥakím:

> Shoghi has kindly supplied me with the correct transliteration of all the Persian and Arabic words and names which occur in my book.[194]

On Monday, 18 October Shoghi Effendi wrote to an oriental believer:

> My dear spiritual friend . . . God be praised, I am in good health and full of hope and trying to the best of my ability to equip myself for those things I shall require in my future service to the Cause. My hope is that I may speedily acquire the best that this country and this society have to offer and then return to my home and recast the truths of the Faith in a new form, and thus serve the Holy Threshold.[195]

The dedication of Shoghi Effendi to the service of the Cause and his vigilance not to miss any opportunity of service are evident from these letters.

Shoghi Effendi officially matriculated in the Non-Collegiate Delegacy on 23 October 1920, just over a week after starting his lectures in the Michaelmas term. The official records show him registered as Showqí Rabbání, Persian, recommended by Lindsay and the Master. Shoghi Effendi's name appears in the Non-Collegiate directory between two students, Mír Maqbúl Mahmúd and William Morris Tudor. His course of study is stated on his matriculation documents as 'Economics & Social Sciences'. The same document gives a list of four lectures for which he had registered in the Michaelmas term. The lectures were: Social and Political Questions given by the Master of Balliol, Social and Industrial

87

Questions given by Rev. Carlyle, Elementary Economics given by Penson, and Political Science also given by Carlyle.[196] During the Michaelmas term Ali Yazdi sent a cable to Shoghi Effendi to inform him of his forthcoming trip to the United States. Shoghi Effendi immediately telegraphed his friend, 'You don't mean to tell me you are going to America without coming to see me.' Ali Yazdi sent Shoghi Effendi a note about his travel to the United States via London to which Shoghi Effendi responded on a postcard dated 3 November 1920 from 45 Broad Street:

> My dear 'Alí,
>   When I received your telegram, I wondered to what address I should forward my answer. Now that I have been informed I hasten to tell you how glad I would be to meet you, shake hands with you, and perform the ceremony of *muṣáfiḥih*.[197] I am bound with my lectures and courses and feel sometimes depressed. I shall be your host when you come to see me. I don't know how you have managed for your travelling expenses.
>   On Thursday and Friday a brilliant debating soc. and an address by Bryce will be delivered.
>   Shoghi[198]

In response to this invitation Ali Yazdi travelled to Oxford and stayed in Shoghi Effendi's room for a couple of nights. Shoghi Effendi took Ali all over the university and showed him the sights. The two friends talked about their difficulties and discussed their preparation for future services to the Cause. Ali Yazdi discussed his financial condition with Shoghi Effendi and expressed his concern about his ability to save enough money to pursue his education. Shoghi Effendi comforted him and extended warm hospitality to this childhood friend.[199]

As Shoghi Effendi was intensely interested in outstanding speakers, especially those who spoke at the Oxford Union, he wanted to take Ali to hear the address by James Bryce and discuss it together afterwards. However, Ali could not stay and had to return to London.

After this visit, Shoghi Effendi sent Ali a note dated 6 November 1920 on an Oxford Union Society card:

> Dear 'Alí:
> I have received your card, and I knew well that it would be difficult for you to come here again. I did miss you profoundly last night and the night before, particularly as I firmly anticipated that we would both enjoy and comment upon the procedures of the debate and lecture. I trust, however, that you will not be detained a long time and that you will not have any difficulties to surmount. I have written to Grandmother about you reminding her of your difficult and strained situation yet your patience and will. I hope that some help might issue by the time you prepare yourself for entrance into college. My best and tenderest wishes be with you always. May we meet again under better circumstances![200]

Despite his own overwhelming problems, Shoghi Effendi could not ignore his friend's financial need. He had empathized with his friend before but could not forget Ali's financial problems. Four days later, on 10 November 1920, he wrote to Ali again:

> Dear 'Alí:
> I really never realized how minute, intense, and urgent were your financial needs. I hasten, therefore, to send you all that I can for the present – namely, five English pounds banknote, which I enclose in this letter. I hope you are staying at Miss Herrick's. She has some rooms to offer to friends who come to London. If you are not there, do apply. She is so kind.

My studies and preoccupations are exerting an effect
upon me almost as distressing as your own difficulties.
Believe me it is so. I don't know what I shall do at the end.
Yours lovingly
Shoghi

For Heaven's sake think not of sending me back anything.
I flatly refuse and decline. Let your mind be at rest.[201]

Shoghi Effendi's difficulty was related to his studies. The
question of his admission to Balliol College was no less
distressing than Ali Yazdi's financial situation. Furthermore,
Shoghi Effendi was extremely busy during this period. He
was so fully engaged in his work that he had little time to
correspond with the Bahá'í friends. Dr Esslemont wrote to
Luṭfu'lláh Ḥakím on Friday 10 December 1920:

I have not heard from Shoghi for some time. I must write
him soon. I heard that he intended going to Glasgow during
his x-mas vacations.[202]

Several letters were exchanged between the College and Mr
Baker, the Censor of the Non-Collegiate Delegacy, after the
end of the Michaelmas term. These letters shed some light
on the discussions behind the scenes between the College and
the Non-Collegiate Delegacy. They highlight the painful
experience Shoghi Effendi endured in dealing with the
college administration.

The Master of Balliol was aware that Shoghi Effendi might
not be allowed to move or migrate into Balliol College in the
second term because of the migration rule. Concerned about
Shoghi Effendi's condition, he himself became involved.[203]

The decision was finally made to admit Shoghi Effendi
into Balliol College during the first week of the winter vacation and this was communicated to Mr Baker through Cyril
Bailey, a Fellow of Balliol College responsible for administration. The Master of Balliol mentioned to Shoghi Effendi's

tutor, Lindsay, that Bailey had discussed Shoghi Effendi's situation with Baker. On 20 December 1920 Lindsay wrote to Baker from his vacation residence in London explaining the background of the situation. He asked Baker to make an exception and allow Shoghi Effendi to migrate to Balliol for the Hilary term even though the rules for migration had not been followed, that is, notice for migration had not been given in the sixth week of the Michaelmas term.

On 22 December Lindsay wrote Baker again responding to a letter he had just received from him about Shoghi Effendi. Lindsay said that he thought Shoghi Effendi was in London and would be making an effort to get hold of Baker. He said that he had told Shoghi Effendi that he would write Baker much earlier. In an apologetic tone, Lindsay blamed himself and was 'very sorry indeed' for not having taken the time to discuss the issue with Baker earlier. He concluded the letter saying, 'I have a great belief in him which has been confirmed from what I have seen of him.'[204]

This positive statement of Lindsay helped Baker correct an earlier impression of Shoghi Effendi that was based purely on reports Baker had received from an informant suggesting that Shoghi Effendi had kept aloof from Oxford social life. In a letter to Lindsay dated 31 December 1920 Baker admitted that his impression of Shoghi Effendi was based on erroneous information he had received from an informant who had mixed up Shoghi Effendi with another person. Baker confirmed that in fact Shoghi Effendi was active in the social life of Oxford. He 'played football and took part in the debates'. Baker admitted that he had somewhat 'wronged the man'.[205]

In the same letter Baker mentioned that he had seen Shoghi Effendi the previous day, Thursday, 30 December, and had told him the news that an application would be submitted to the Delegacy for his migration into Balliol on 15 January and that there was no reason for it to be refused.

Baker was confident that Shoghi Effendi's certificate of migration would be issued on Monday, 17 January 1921.[206]

Upon receipt of Baker's letter, Lindsay felt that he should correct Shoghi Effendi's records at Balliol College. He wrote a note to Cyril Bailey on Thursday, 6 January 1921 informing him that the unkind remarks made about Shoghi Effendi had not been true. His note to Bailey also shows that in the second term, Shoghi Effendi was to write a paper on the 'Republic and Ethics' and on 'History of Philosophy from Descartes to Kant'.[207]

On 15 January 1921 permission was issued by the Non-Collegiate Delegacy for the migration of Shoghi Effendi into Balliol. Two days later Shoghi Effendi received a certificate of migration signed by two proctors. Thus, he officially migrated to Balliol and signed the college Register, as the 1st son of Mírzá Hádí Shírází, age 23.[208]

12

Hilary Term in Balliol

Shoghi Effendi started the Hilary term 1921 as an official Balliol student living in college, occupying a room in one of its western buildings. The room provided sleeping, study and entertainment areas. Shoghi Effendi studied in his room and in the Balliol college library as well as in the Oxford University Bodleian Library. The buildings of the college served as a wall surrounding it on three sides and a wall separated Balliol from the neighbouring Trinity College. A porter's lodge was by the college gate, which was locked at night. From the college Shoghi Effendi could walk to the important buildings of the university. Below is a brief description of the main college areas that Shoghi Effendi would have visited on a daily basis.

College Main Gate and Front Quadrangle

The layout of the porter's lodge area today is different from that seen by Shoghi Effendi in 1920. Upon entering the gate, the area immediately to the right used to have a door through which the students entered to receive their mail and to sign the porter's register. That entrance has now been replaced with a wall. After entering through the gate, one sees the front quadrangle.

The front quadrangle dates back to the 14th century and constitutes the oldest part of the college. Every part of the quadrangle has been restored several times in its long history.

Surrounding the front quadrangle is a range of buildings that includes students' living quarters.

College Library

The building on the west of the front quadrangle used to be the Old Hall where students had their meals. However, in 1853 the hall was converted to a library. In 1920 Shoghi Effendi would have spent many hours in this library, the entrance to which was near the Master's Lodgings. In 1920 the present entrance and floor did not exist.

Garden Quadrangle

This area is the newer part of the college and comprises a garden surrounded by the staircases. The formal building bordering it dates back to the 18th century. There are several buildings which Shoghi Effendi would have visited and these are described below in a clockwise circuit of the perimeter.

The Master's Lodgings

These were constructed in 1867 when the Master of Balliol was Robert Scott. In 1920, the then Master, A.L. Smith occupied these quarters. He would have received Shoghi Effendi here.

Staircases X through XIV

These staircases, which are known respectively as the Fisher's Building, the Bristol Building and Basevi's Building, occupy the south and just over two-thirds of the western edge of the garden quadrangle. They were constructed between 1759 and 1826. Shoghi Effendi probably visited several of his friends in these staircases.

Junior Common Room

This building was erected in 1912. The Junior Common Room occupied the ground floor and the basement of the building. The main room was extended and remodelled in 1964. Shoghi Effendi used the common room for after-dinner teas and discussions. The style and decoration of the room, however, have changed since Shoghi Effendi's sojourn in Oxford.

Salvin's Buildings

These buildings, which constitute staircases XVI to XVIII, were designed by Salvin in 1853. They replaced earlier college buildings including the Master's stables and a building known as Caesar's Lodgings. The back gate of the college, previously located next to the Junior Common Room, was relocated in its present position and a tower constructed above it at the same time. This door opened to St Giles and is opposite Beaumont Street.

Shoghi Effendi's room was most probably in the Salvin's building. He had indicated to the friends that his window opened to the Martyrs' Memorial.

The Hall

The Hall was built in 1877 and has since been used for serving meals to the students and faculty. It contains rows of tables with benches on each side. The High Table, where the Master, Fellows and tutors dine, is situated along the opposite end of the Hall from the entrance and is set perpendicular to the other tables. The windows in the Hall were originally fully glazed. In 1910 panelling was installed inside and the lower sections were blocked up. The Hall is decorated by brightly painted heraldic decorations related to benefactors. Large portraits of the Masters of Balliol College as well as of

95

distinguished alumni create a serious atmosphere. The Hall is where Shoghi Effendi would have eaten his meals every day while in college.

The East Side and Lawn

The buildings that stand on the northeast side of Balliol College adjacent to the Hall did not exist when Shoghi Effendi was at Balliol. The east side had a wall separating it from Trinity College. Inside the wall was a garden with gordouli and mulberry trees.

The Fellows' Garden

This area, a charming garden, faces the Old Common Room and was used by the Fellows of the college. It was enclosed and had a passage on its west side.

Holywell Annexe

In 1920 Balliol College had an annexe which was used by students during their vacations. Surrounding the annexe were sports grounds, including tennis courts, where students played single or double matches with their friends.[209]

Shoghi Effendi in College

The first week of the Hilary term ended on 27 January. Shoghi Effendi was in college during this week. The record of his expenses in Balliol College shows charges in the categories 'kitchen', 'stores' and 'messenger'. The kitchen charge refers to the meals served in the dining hall for the week and was £1/16/6 (one pound, 16 shillings and six pence). The stores charge refers to supplies Shoghi Effendi bought in the college stores and was 2/9 (two shillings and nine pence). The messenger charge probably refers to the fee for delivering messages within Oxford and shows an amount of four pence.[210]

The students of Balliol College had observed Shoghi Effendi in the college grounds during the first term. However, at that time he was a student attempting to be admitted into college. When he was admitted, they were curious to know who he was. The rumour was that Shoghi Effendi was related to the head of the Bahá'í Faith and would be occupying a high position in the Faith.

It is certain that the attitudes of students during this time at Oxford were class conscious. The attitudes were reinforced by an institution that was conscious of its own destiny to produce the leaders of tomorrow in a sheltered, intellectual atmosphere rooted firmly in the past. These attitudes prevail even today. For example, on a spring Sunday afternoon, one can still observe young men punting on the Cherwell River, spending considerable time reading newspapers and taking tea in the Junior Common Room or JCR, as it is called. One notices how these young men pride themselves on their wit, on *what* they say as well as *how* they say it. One finds students listening intently with upraised eyebrows and polite *hmmms* to the discourses around them, portraying a facade of effortless superiority. These attitudes were prevalent in 1920 and the recollections of Shoghi Effendi's contemporaries may be better understood in the context of such class-conscious attitudes.

Many of the students did not take the opportunity to spend time with Shoghi Effendi or get to know him. They observed him from a distance. Shoghi Effendi's zeal, his loftiness of purpose, his seriousness about the goal he had set for himself and his diligence in all facets of his work surprised many students who believed that a Balliol man should show his 'superiority' without appearing to be making any effort. Most other students would conceal the amount of work they had put into their assignments in order to show that their work had been completed with little effort. Boyce Gibson, one of Shoghi Effendi's contemporaries, refers to this attitude of the upper-class English students of this period:

> I wonder how much he [Shoghi Effendi] liked his experience at Balliol. I doubt if he really felt at home there. It was not a matter of being Asian: Some of the Indians who were up with me were thoroughly at home there. Possibly it was that he knew he had a mission to fulfil, and in letting it be known he both cut across the current mood of benevolent incredulity and flouted the upper-class English convention of the time, that one should not <u>appear</u> to take things too seriously. I fear that he was sometimes hoaxed and I still don't know whether he was aware of it.[211]

As time passed, the students began to see Shoghi Effendi in a different light. They observed him in a variety of situations: discussing issues with enthusiasm in the dining hall, in the Junior Common Room (JCR), attending the Oxford Union debates and discussing the debate with fellow students. Through these interactions Shoghi Effendi's popularity grew. He became well respected and admired by the majority of students.

The records of his college expenses show his increasing social activity in the college. During the third, fourth and fifth weeks of the Hilary term, the college weekly expense record shows charges made by Shoghi Effendi for 'JCR teas', referring to afternoon teas and sandwiches which Shoghi Effendi probably bought for himself and his guests. In the third, fifth, sixth and seventh weeks of the term, his weekly expense sheet shows charges for 'gate bill', which refers to the charge for entering the college gate after it was closed at 9 p.m.[212]

While the subjects Shoghi Effendi was studying in Oxford were of interest to him, his primary purpose was to prepare himself for his future services to the Cause by perfecting his

English so that he might be able to translate adequately the sacred writings of the Faith. To a friend in London he wrote:

> I am engaged in this land, day and night, in perfecting myself in the area of translation . . . I do not have a moment's rest. Thank God that to some extent at least the results are good.[213]

In a letter written on Friday, 28 January 1921 from Balliol College to a Persian friend, Shoghi Effendi expressed his happiness for having just completed the translation of the Persian Hidden Words and the Tablet of Visitation. He had also translated other Tablets and letters of the Master and was happy that to some degree he had rendered a service to the Holy Threshold. He expressed the hope that in the near future the Súriy-i-Haykal and the Tablets to the Kings would be translated in the most perfect, the most novel and the most eloquent style, thus demonstrating a clear evidence that would justify his remoteness from the holy court. He sent greetings to the friends of the region, particularly to Mírzá Dáwúd and Dr Aflátún.[214]

Shoghi Effendi sent some of the translated Tablets, together with essays he had written, to a few of the English friends for their comments and corrections of the English. The individuals who had the bounty of receiving these early translations and essays were Dr Esslemont, Lady Blomfield and Miss Rosenberg.

In an undated letter written on Balliol College stationary to Lady Blomfield, who was often addressed as Sitárih Khánum, a title given to her by the Master, Shoghi Effendi wrote about his translation work:

> I shall send you my version of the Arabic Hidden Words & the Epistle to Queen Victoria as soon as they are ready and I hope to have the pleasure of receiving any remarks or corrections you may desire to make with regard to them . . .

As I desire to submit my paper on the Cause to Dr Carpenter[215] I would be much obliged if you could return it when convenient.[216]

On 5 February 1921 Dr Esslemont wrote to Dr Luṭfu'lláh Ḥakím:

> I had a letter from Shoghi this week. He seems to be very busy at Oxford, and more satisfied than he was last session.[217]

Shoghi Effendi wrote to Dr Esslemont on 17 February 1921 acknowledging the receipt of the essay Dr Esslemont had corrected and sharing the news that he had been asked to read a paper on the Bahá'í movement at the Oxford University Asiatic Society, which represented twelve nationalities:

> I have gladly accepted & have a long, comprehensive and elaborate paper which I hope to read this Monday. It is a custom of the Society to invite at every meeting an official of the University or an outsider who will be fully acquainted with the subject under discussion & who will address the society after or before the discussion is made on the paper.
>
> I understand that the Society has requested Dr Estlin Carpenter to act as their distinguished visitor on that occasion but he seems to have been unable to respond to their invitation. They have now written to Prof. Browne & presumably they have intimated to him the nature of the subject & the name of the speaker. I presume he will be present but notwithstanding the attitude he will probably take in the discussion I have decided not to modify the tone of my speech & have preserved my quotations of his account when he visited Baha'u'llah in Acre. I don't know what will ensue in the meeting & what will be the atmosphere of the discussion in his presence. It is quite an unexpected turn & we hope for the best.[218]

According to the college records, Shoghi Effendi probably left the college for the spring vacation a day or two before the conclusion of the eighth week of the Hilary term, which ended on 17 March 1921.[219]

13

Spring Vacation 1921

The spring vacation began in mid-March and ended late in April. Shoghi Effendi spent the earlier part of this vacation in Scotland visiting his sister Rúḥangíz. The latter part of the vacation was spent in Sussex. This is stated in a letter written by Dr Esslemont to Luṭfu'lláh Ḥakím, dated 23 March 1921.[220]

Although Shoghi Effendi was extremely busy during this vacation and barely spent time in Oxford, yet spring was the season he would begin to play tennis, a game he loved and in which he excelled. He played tennis with many students during this season as well as in the summer.

One of his tennis partners, J. C. Hill, gives a picture of Shoghi Effendi's speed in hitting the ball and his enjoyment of the game:

> I used to play tennis with him in the Master's Field, and marvellously active he was . . . He was ambidextrous and switched his racket from one hand to the other for a volley or the net with lightning speed – but not in a grimly earnest manner. On the contrary he was laughing . . . most of the time.[221]

Geoffrey Meade, another Balliol student who played tennis with Shoghi Effendi, has left this description:

> He was very keen to hit vigorously at the ball, which either went out or into the net, or was a brilliant shot. When serv-

ing he would go as far back as possible and serve as he strode briskly forward. If his ball went out or into the net he would stride on, as often as not coming well inside the service line before sending the second ball. When 'fault' was called he thought it a great joke, and it is a tribute to his popularity that it was a joke in which his partner shared.[222]

Adrian Franklin remembers not only playing tennis with Shoghi Effendi but also the quality of the courts:

> I distinctly remember playing tennis with him on the very bad Balliol clay courts: he had a very hard service for so short a man. Am I right in thinking he played left handed?[223]

We also have the recollection of G. Raleigh, who claims to have defeated Shoghi Effendi at a tennis match:

> Curiously enough, I happen to recall quite well that last time I played with him, I had the good luck to beat him quite soundly – 6–2, 6–1, or something like that. We enjoyed our games together, because we enjoyed tennis in very much the same way. He was such a pleasant person to play with.[224]

We also have the recollection of J. C. Dwyer, a student who had come to Balliol one year before Shoghi Effendi. He paints a picture of the fearless spirit of Shoghi Effendi:

> An example of his intrepid spirit, I remember hearing of him that he had addressed Hopkins, an American Rhodes Scholar, with the words: 'Hopkins! I hear that you are a Tennis Blue. Let us have a game sometimes.'[225]

These recollections add to the picture we have of the serious young Shoghi Effendi and show his sense of humour, his love for sports and his friendship with his contemporaries. Some of the tennis matches described could have taken place during this spring vacation, despite the fact that Shoghi Effendi was away from Oxford most of the time.

On Tuesday, 29 March 1921 Shoghi Effendi wrote from Scotland to Ḍíyá'u'lláh Aṣgharzádih stating that he had arrived a few days earlier to see his sister and attend to her affairs. Ḍíyá'u'lláh Aṣgharzádih, who received numerous letters from Shoghi Effendi, was a Persian believer born in Mílán in 1880. He had made pilgrimage to the Holy Land twice, in 1903 and 1920. During his second pilgrimage, he spent several months in the presence of the Master. After this pilgrimage he went to London where he carried on business as carpet merchant.[226]

In his letter to Ḍíyá'u'lláh Aṣgharzádih Shoghi Effendi expressed his hope to go to London a few days later to meet the friends and to attend spiritual meetings in the home of Mírzá Yúhaná Dáwúd, which was located in a secluded and quiet area. He mentioned that in Glasgow there was an Indian youth who had recently been blessed with a Tablet from the Master and that he hoped to meet this young man before proceeding to London.[227]

The Master, knowing Shoghi Effendi's earlier physical condition as well as his diligence and drive, had sent clear instructions that Shoghi Effendi should spend some days resting. Shoghi Effendi obeyed the Master's wishes and spent a few days during this vacation in Fermore Villa in Sussex, which had a good climate, to engage in prayers, meditation and services to the Cause.[228]

Although he was on holiday and away from his studies, Shoghi Effendi was busily engaged making translations, giving him rest only from his academic work. On Monday, 16 April 1921 Shoghi Effendi wrote a letter from Sussex to a Persian friend enclosing a Tablet he had just received from the Master stating that he had been engaged in the translation work in Sussex for the previous two days. However, having forgotten to bring along with him from Oxford several important Tablets, he wished this friend to immediately mail him copies of the Tablets of Ṭarázát and Bishárát or the blue book Shaykh Faraj had published. He stressed that he needed these Tablets urgently and was awaiting them.[229]

On Wednesday, 20 April 1921 Shoghi Effendi was back in Oxford. He again wrote his Persian friend indicating that the notebook containing some Tablets had arrived. He wrote that he was taking extracts from the Tablets and returning them. He was, he said, immersed in translation work. In the two days since his return to Oxford, he had, on instructions of 'Abdu'l-Bahá, translated some general Tablets, prayers and the Tablet of Tajallíyát.[230]

14

Trinity Term 1921

Balliol College records for the first week of Trinity term ending 28 April 1921 show Shoghi Effendi's full participation in all college activities. He took his meals in the college dining hall, purchased items in the college stores, used the college messenger services and paid one shilling for bicycle repair. He spent nine full weeks in college during the Trinity term, excepting probably a day or two prior to the conclusion of the ninth week ending 23 June 1921.[231]

The Trinity term had hardly begun when Shoghi Effendi began planning ahead for the summer. To ensure he would not waste a moment of the long vacation that would soon follow, he sought a competent tutor to work with him during the summer months. His first choice was Nicholson, the Arabic scholar. On Friday, 29 April 1921 Shoghi Effendi wrote to Miss Rosenberg:

> I hope your efforts will bear fruit and a satisfactory arrangement will be entered with Nicholson as I more and more feel that he is the only fitting and competent person for the job.
>
> If that fails I don't see how I can properly and profitably spend my long vacation. Would Miss Cropper be able to arrange my work with Nicholson? I am so anxious to do some tangible substantial work during the long vacation.
>
> I am working on philosophy with Mr Lindsay & on English with two Balliol tutors, one of them admirably competent in English. What I need this vacation is direct help & correction of my translations . . . an English stylist

would not be desirable if he has no knowledge of Persian or
Arabic.

The Tajaliat, Ishraqat, Glad Tidings have been completed. I am now filling my leisure hours working at the
Epistle to the Shah & the Suratul-Haykal.[232]

On Friday, 29 April 1921 Shoghi Effendi wrote a letter to a
Persian friend in response to an invitation to attend the
Riḍván gathering of the friends. He indicated that the strict
rules of the college prevented him from leaving the city and
therefore he regretted that he was not able to attend such a
joyous Riḍván occasion. Otherwise, he asked, who would
prefer seclusion in such a place and during such joyous times
to the fellowship with the friends of God? However, he continued, it was certain that, God willing, living in remote
regions and in isolation would be followed by worthy services
to the Cause of God; and this loneliness would be followed
by the closeness and good pleasure of God.[233]

One of the objectives Shoghi Effendi had stated in his
application to Oxford University was to associate with 'cultured and refined people'. Shoghi Effendi was able to accomplish this goal after his migration into Balliol. He associated
with a large number of students who had an extremely high
respect for him despite the fact that he was not British and
did not conform to the upper-class British convention. As
mentioned above, many assumed he would in future be the
head of the Bahá'í Faith. Among his group of friends were
B. J. Bevan-Petman, Paul Leroy-Beaulieu, Boyce Gibson,
William Y. Elliot, Leonard Manyon and J. R. Cullen. With
these friends he played tennis and conversed on philosophical and religious issues, always with high excitement. C. C.
Greer stated:

I recall that we knew him to be somehow destined to head
the Baha'i Faith – a fact which made him an interesting and
unusual figure in the College.[234]

Mr Soskice, a contemporary of Shoghi Effendi, also provided his impressions:

> I certainly remember that he was very friendly and easy to get on with and enjoyed laughter and conversation. He was not in the least aloof and liked making friends . . . I have an impression of him rather restless, moving about a good deal and not often to be seen sitting down for any prolonged period.[235]

Shoghi Effendi left a profound impression on some of the students at Balliol. Like many others, A. W. Davis remembered him after 50 years:

> As it was, however, ours was little more than a casual acquaintance, yet even that was enough for me to remember Rabbani quite distinctly after nearly fifty years when I have forgotten even the names of almost all my contemporaries at Balliol. There was always something 'different' about him.[236]

This account by B. H. Bevan-Petman describes the respect Shoghi Effendi commanded:

> Rabbani, yes, of course I remember him.
> Rabbani was irrepressibly cheerful, always on the point of laughter, and bouncing around . . . Wherever he was, spirits were high. We all knew him destined for spiritual leadership: and believe me, in no sense of irreverence or discourtesy, he was affectionately known as 'God'. (Naughty but inevitable!)[237]

A similar account is provided by another Balliol man of that time, Geoffrey Meade:

> We were of course aware at Balliol of his high position in the Bahá'í Faith and he was affectionately referred to as 'The

God Kid'. I say affectionately because there was no hint of mockery in this – he was far too well liked for that . . .

In conclusion I would say that not only I but all at Balliol liked him very much & esteemed him & were very sorry when he left after so short a stay.[238]

J. C. Hills remembered the time he spent with Shoghi Effendi:

> He used to walk, punt, meet after Hall in various people's rooms. S. P. Streuve and D. W. Lascelles were often there. In Shoghi's room there could be Russian Caravan tea . . . to be drunk, he insisted, with Cardamon seeds. He gave me a pair of Giveh[239] I had for years, which had been sent by his family with many other things. He loved to quote Hafiz and Saadi. I got the love of Persian Poetry from him.[240]

S. P. Streuve spent much time with Shoghi Effendi and had the honour of receiving an inscription, a prayer in Arabic, from him:

> During the short period of time when we were both at Balliol (I went down in 1921) we talked with each other quite often . . . for some reason he conceived a liking for me or took an interest in me . . . I seem to remember that I also attended Dr Carlyle's lecture in Political Science . . . Perhaps some light on his attitude to me will be thrown by the enclosed xerox copy of the inscription he made for me, just before leaving Oxford, on a piece of parchment-like paper. When I asked him to translate for me what he wrote there he refused to do so. I think he said that perhaps one day I would learn the language and be able to read it for myself . . .[241]

The illustrations show two passages from the writings of Bahá'u'lláh penned in Shoghi Effendi's superb handwriting.

109

The translation of the passage appearing horizontally is as follows:

> He is God
> My hair is My Attributes – in which My Beauty is Concealed! Perchance the Eyes of the strangers from among My servants may fall on it, thus have We hidden from the infidels the Beauty which is Shining and Exalted.[242]

The translation of the vertical lines is as follows:

> He is the Mighty, the Beloved
> My Lock is My Chain – whosoever clings to it shall never err from everlasting to everlasting, for therein is hidden the Guidance which leads to Light of Beauty.[243]

To gain insight into the meaning of these passages, one should refer to other Tablets of Bahá'u'lláh where the metaphor of the hair is used, such as in the prayer for the Fast.[244]

Shoghi Effendi was asked to present a paper to the Lotus Club. This club provided a forum for the discussion of intellectual issues. Two of his contemporaries, J. P. de Menasce and William Elliot, refer to the paper he presented to this club. Elliot writes:

> Shoghi Rabbani, or simply Rabbani as he was more often called, was so retiring that he did not lend himself to very much discussion, even though his points of view in religion were certainly very deep and appeared from time to time in such discussion clubs as I remember taking him to. The Lotus Club principally was the outstanding club, I think, for intellectual discussion and dialogue . . . The Lotus Club appreciated the qualities of Rabbani.[245]

In her book *The Priceless Pearl* Rúḥíyyih Khánum quotes a letter from Shoghi Effendi to a believer confirming that he

Main gate to Balliol College, Broad Street

Through the Broad Street gate

St Giles entrance to Balliol College

Through the St Giles gate

The Martyrs' Memorial, St Giles

Balliol Library

The Master's Lodgings, where Shoghi Effendi met with A. L. Smith

The Junior Common Room, where Shoghi Effendi met fellow students

The Hall, where Shoghi Effendi had his meals

The interior of the Hall

Shoghi Effendi, standing centre, among students at Balliol College

An inscription written by Shoghi Effendi for a friend at Balliol

Letter written by Shoghi Effendi from Balliol College

Shoghi Effendi with Bahá'ís in Manchester, October 1921

Shoghi Effendi, Guardian of the Bahá'í Faith, 1922

presented a paper to one of the societies at Oxford. This could have been the Lotus Club or another club:

> I shall also later send you a paper on the Movement which I read some time ago at one of the leading societies in Oxford.[246]

Shoghi Effendi also presented papers to the Bahá'í community in London, as this letter from an Indian believer indicates:

> On Wednesday evening [4 May 1921] I went to attend the usual Bahá'í meeting at Lindsay Hall. Mr Shoghi Rabbani read a paper dealing with the economic problems and their solution. His paper was beautifully worded and was very good . . .[247]

On 12 May 1921 Shoghi Effendi wrote to a Persian believer, probably Díyá'u'lláh Aşgharzádih, asking him to send back papers which he had earlier sent to be read in the company of the friends. He mentioned that he needed these papers for his future conversations with some of the notables of Oxford University.[248]

111

15

Long Vacation 1921

The long vacation started in the third week of June and continued until the first week in October. Miss Edna True, who had met Shoghi Effendi in Haifa in 1919, wrote this account of her meeting with him in London at the beginning of the vacation.

> In June . . . when I knew I was going to London, I wrote the Guardian offering to go to Oxford to see him. He replied that he would be passing through London at that very time . . . and suggesting that we have tea together at my hotel.
>
> While we were having tea, in this rather large salon of the hotel, word was sent to me that Captain so-and-so was at the reception desk with my plane ticket over to France. The Guardian spoke up and requested that the Captain be brought to us, and when he arrived, seemed most interested in my flight, asking just where my seat was. On looking over the plan of the plane, he noticed an open cock-pit in front of the pilot's cabin, and he asked the Captain if I could not have a place there. The captain replied that passengers did not usually sit there, but he promised to do what he could about it, and when I arrived at the airfield, he appeared with the news that I had to put on a special helmet, goggles, etc.! All of this had been the Guardian's idea and wish, but it proved to be an exciting experience.[249]

During the long vacation Balliol students wishing to study during the summer moved from the college to an annexe situated near Manchester College known as the Holywell

Annexe. Shoghi Effendi stayed in this annexe for a part of this long vacation. One of his contemporaries, L. Forbes-Ritte, referred to the time he spent with Shoghi Effendi in this annexe:

> He was quiet, agile minded, singularly well informed about this country, and that I attribute to his always wanting to know why . . . He did spend a few weeks with Abdu'l-Hamid and me in a Holywell annexe we had. It was used in the long vac. by those wishing to stay up for study. We three, so far as I can recall, breakfasted together each day, and as the only 'native' I leg-pulled a great deal, when they asked questions.[250]

G. E. Lavin, who had come up to Balliol in 1918, described a conversation he had with Shoghi Effendi during this vacation:

> I have clear recollections of several hours' discussion with him in the Quad one summer's evening when we debated a number of broad ethical problems and found we had much in common although our backgrounds were very different.[251]

Sometime before the first week of July Shoghi Effendi left Oxford. His exact itinerary is not known. We do know, however, that on 6 July 1921 Dr Esslemont received a letter from him in which he stated that he would be visiting Dr Esslemont for a few days in a fortnight's time. Dr Esslemont mentioned this in a letter to Dr Ḥakím postmarked 7 July 1921. He also states that Shoghi Effendi was in Crowborough, Sussex, during the university vacation.[252]

On 9 July 1921 Shoghi Effendi wrote to Miss Rosenberg thanking her for her kindness in forwarding his correspondence and sharing his immediate plans for the vacation. He states that he was planning to leave the next day for Bournemouth and would stay there for about two weeks. On

26 July he came to London to meet his sister and went with her to Mrs Thornburgh-Cropper's. Regarding his work and translations he wrote:

> My work with my tutor has been successfully terminated & among other Tablets, the Epistle to Nap. III has been carefully & properly translated. I hope to share it with you when I meet you next in London.[253]

On 10 August 1921 Shoghi Effendi was in Torquay. He wrote in Persian to Ḍíyá'u'lláh Aṣgharzádih from 115 Abbey Road. In this letter he states that the Master had given instructions that he was to abstain from work, studies and meetings and was to rest outside London. This point had been repeatedly emphasized by the Centre of the Cause. Therefore, after consultation with Mrs [Thornburgh-] Cropper and Major Tudor-Pole, Shoghi Effendi was spending some time in Torquay. He hoped to make a trip with Ḍíyá'u'lláh to Manchester at the end of the vacation. He had heard of the devotion of the Manchester friends to the Centre of the Covenant.[254]

The next day, 11 August 1921, Shoghi Effendi wrote to Miss Rosenberg again:

> I am delighted with the exquisite Tablet you have received & I am afraid my modest version has failed to convey the charm & force of the original. One doubtful word in the text, I have inserted suspension mark, & which I may discover if you tell me what its rendering has been in the original translation – I have taken the liberty to transcribe a copy both of the original and my version & shall be much obliged if you would let me know, as soon as convenient, all your suggestions as to my version that I may revise my own copy accordingly. Your remarks touching my version of the daily prayer, are most welcome & I am surprised to know that there is such a fitting equivalent in the Bible as the render of heavens.[255]

On Monday, 29 August 1921 Shoghi Effendi wrote a letter from Torquay to Ḍíyá'u'lláh Aṣgharzádih acknowledging receipt of his letter and saying how much he had enjoyed reading it, for it demonstrated his dedication to the Cause. In the Torquay region, he wrote, one could not sense the fragrance of spirituality as people were immersed in materialism and superstition. He hoped Ḍíyá'u'lláh would travel with him to Manchester at the end of the summer to visit the believers.[256]

To an undated letter to Miss Rosenberg on Balliol stationary, probably written during the latter part of the long vacation in September, Shoghi Effendi attached the translation of a Tablet from the Master. This Tablet had been revealed on 20 August 1921 in honour of Mrs Crossley, praising her for the contribution she had made to the Temple fund and for her self-sacrifice in the path of God:

> My dear Miss Rosenberg:
>   I would be indeed much obliged to you if you could glance at my version of Mrs Crossley's Tablet & make any corrections you deem necessary & return it to me immediately . . . I am asked to send copies of it to some of the friends . . .[257]

Mrs Crossley was a devoted Bahá'í who had responded to the call for contributions for the construction of the House of Worship in Wilmette by selling her beautiful hair and sending the proceeds to the Temple Unity fund. Her selfless action had brought joy to the heart of the Master.[258]

In an undated letter written to a Persian friend on Balliol stationary, Shoghi Effendi stated that he had just finished a translation of a sacred Tablet of the Master for Mrs Crossley, which he had sent to her through Mr Hall. He also mentioned that he was engaged in further translations and publications of the Tablets.[259]

115

On Friday, 23 September, Shoghi Effendi wrote to Díyá'u'lláh Asgharzádih praising God that his period of rest had been completed and that the days of study were approaching. In a few days he would arrive in London in order to send his sister to school in Scotland. He wished to meet Díyá'u'lláh so that they might travel together to Manchester before returning to Oxford for the forthcoming term.[260]

On the following Wednesday Shoghi Effendi sent a note to Díyá'u'lláh about going to Manchester on Saturday, 1 October. He said that his sister, who had been staying with Mrs Thornburgh-Cropper, had returned and was on her way to Scotland. Shoghi Effendi would come to Díyá'u'lláh's home the next evening for a visit and to arrange the Manchester trip.[261]

Two days later Shoghi Effendi wrote a letter from 20 Bloomsbury Square, London, to Lady Blomfield expressing his pleasure at having seen her the previous evening and having had a long talk with her. He mentioned that he was planning to go to Manchester the following day and hoped to see her within a week. He also told her of his translation work:

> Your interest in my work of translation has encouraged me a great deal & my hope is that I shall in the near future realize my aspiration of rendering adequately & forcibly the words of Baha'u'llah & the Master into English.
>
> I am enclosing a copy of one of the earliest of Baha'u-'llah's prayers revealed in the early days of his stay in Baghdad. The prayer in Arabic is simply exquisite & I am not sure whether my rendering it into English has any merit whatever & whether it conveys anything of the charm of the original. You may keep it, if you think it worth your while, as I have duplicates of it.
>
> I shall very gladly submit to your kind consideration & criticism my translations of the Epistles to Nap. III & Queen Victoria, of the Book of the Covenant & of other miscella-

neous writings & prayers of Baha'u'llah & the Master, after
I reach Oxford & hope to forward later my version of the
Arabic Hidden Words . . .[262]

Visit to Manchester

Dr Esslemont visited the Bahá'ís of Manchester in late August
1921 and gave them the good news that Shoghi Effendi was
planning a visit to the city in the near future.[263]

The community of believers in Manchester was active and
devoted. The community had its roots in the earliest days of
the Faith in Britain. Edward Theodore Hall, one of the pillars
of the Faith in Manchester, learned of the Faith as early as
1910. He read an article about the brotherhood of man in
the *Christian Commonwealth* and wrote to Major Wellesley
Tudor-Pole, the author of the article, to obtain further information. Major Tudor-Pole forwarded the letter to Ethel
Rosenberg, who sent Bahá'í literature to Mr Hall and put him
in contact with Sarah Ann Ridgeway, the only Bahá'í in
Manchester, who had learned of the Faith in 1899 in Balti-
more. Soon Mr Hall's wife, Rebecca, and her brother, John
Craven, and his wife, Hester, all embraced the Cause of
God.[264]

The Faith grew during the next decade in Manchester to
just over 20 believers, including a young Persian merchant,
Jacob Joseph, who was from a distinguished Jewish background. Mr Joseph offered to hold Bahá'í meetings in his
office in Mosley Street starting in August 1920. This office,
electrically lit and heated, became the gathering place for the
believers.[265]

Shoghi Effendi arrived in Manchester on Saturday,
1 October, eager to meet this community of devoted friends.
He stayed until the following Thursday as the guest of the
Josephs.[266]

On Saturday evening the friends in Manchester gathered
in Mr Joseph's office to await the arrival of Shoghi Effendi.

117

The friends were so anxious to meet him that they were in a state of animation and expectancy when he walked in with Mr Joseph. Edward Hall has described this meeting:

[Shoghi Effendi] made everyone at ease. His eyes were bright, his voice reassuring, his manners perfect, his features beautiful. He was as one, who, having control of himself, would therefore be able to control others. He commanded respect without seeming to know it. His youthfulness attracted us and the brightness of his thoughts called out our admiration. We all became very happy, and led him to the principal chair, and, as he wished to tell us about the Master's pleasure at Mrs Crossley's action, we placed her in the chair next to his.[267]

That evening, Lucy Hall requested that Shoghi Effendi write a few words in her autograph book. Granting this request, Shoghi Effendi wrote the following inscription:

O Divine Providence!
Pitiful are we; grant us Thy succour! Homeless and wanderers; give us Thy shelter! Scattered; do Thou unite us! Astray; join us to the fold! Bereft; do Thou bestow upon us a share and portion! Athirst; lead us to the wellspring of Life! Frail; strengthen us! that we may arise to exalt Thy Cause and present ourselves a living sacrifice in the pathway of guidance!

What can I offer sweeter than the words of the Beloved Master? I trust you will commit them to memory and remember me.

To Miss Lucy Hall from Shoghi Effendi, her brother in Baha'u'llah.[268]

Shoghi Effendi met the friends again the following afternoon, at the same location, and was present at their gathering that evening in the home of Mr and Mrs Heald. The singing of hymns by the friends pleased Shoghi Effendi and reminded

118

him of the days in the Holy Land when Lua Getsinger would sing a hymn for the Master. Shoghi Effendi told the friends that Lua's singing so pleased the Master that He would ask her 'to go out on the terrace of the house at Haifa, in the cool fragrant night . . . and sing the hymn which always pleased Him – "Nearer my God to Thee". Her voice would rise and fall clear as a nightingale's, to the joy of the Master.'[269]

Shoghi Effendi shared with the friends some Persian poems that could be used as hymns. Lucy Hall recalled:

> Shoghi Effendi told me the words of a hymn in Persian and he asked me for a hymn tune to fit. I played 'The Old Hundredth' from C. of E. *Hymns Ancient and Modern*. I can only remember the first two lines and do not know Persian but here they are, if you can translate them: 'Sínáy-i-haq pur núr shud; vádíy-i-muqadas túr shud . . .'[270]

These words are from the writings of 'Abdu'l-Bahá and give the glad tidings of the new revelation of God that has once again illuminated the Sinai of the Lord.

The next day, Monday, 3 October, Shoghi Effendi and Ḍíyá'u'lláh Aṣgharzádih visited the Hall family. Shoghi Effendi presented to them a photograph of the Master on which he inscribed a few words. He then expressed his love for the children and gave them each a Persian name.[271]

Later in the afternoon, Mr Hall took Shoghi Effendi and Ḍíyá'u'lláh to the house of the Reverend H.H. Johnson, in Cheetham Hills. Johnson had heard of the Cause when 'Abdu'l-Bahá had been in London in 1911. His reading of Bahá'í books and his search had led him to the Unitarian ministry. He told Shoghi Effendi that he had written an article on the Bahá'í Faith and had submitted it to the Master. He was happy that this article had been published in the *Times Educational Supplement*.[272]

Following this visit Shoghi Effendi joined the friends for the evening at Mr Joseph's office. He chanted a prayer and

119

later shared some purple grapes he had bought earlier at a fruit stand on his way to Mosley Street. During the meeting, Shoghi Effendi showed the friends a small bottle of attar of rose which the Greatest Holy Leaf had given him and instructed him to share with the friends when moved by the spiritual atmosphere of a meeting.[273] Here is Lucy Hall's recollection of that evening nearly 50 years later:

> I can still remember quite clearly standing in the room with him whilst he explained to me how it was the quintessence and how this was made. The perfume lingered well over twenty years on the handkerchiefs and in the box in which they were treasured.[274]

Edward Hall also remembered the event:

> He asked us each to hold out a hand, palm upwards, and as he passed around the room he placed a little of this quintessence of rose-fragrance upon it; then we each, following the example of Joseph . . . rubbed our hands together and stroked our palms over our hair and forehead, until ourselves and the whole atmosphere were deliciously fragrant. Then he told us beautiful things of the great Fellowship and tender things of the Holy Places, until we were no longer in Manchester, but rather in the spirit of the Holy Land.[275]

That evening, the friends were moved to write the following supplication to the Master:

Our dear Lord and loving Master,

    At this moment when we are full of joy that we have attained to the meeting with thy richly illumined, beautiful, and radiant grandson, Shoghi Effendi, and have become re-inspired and re-invigorated by the pure flame of his love and his message to us, the strength of which is reinforced by the pure spirit of his honor, [Ḍíyá'u'lláh] (whose every thought and act is in Thy service), we append our humble signatures to this earnest appeal for Thy supplications on our behalf – who are so small and insignificant in the midst of this great city, which is in such need of the Love of God. We are beginners in the school of the Word of God; we are attracted to the Blessed Perfection through the teachings of 'Abdu'l-Bahá, and we have turned our faces to His Glory.

We know that all Thou doest is for our own good and for the good of the world, and in the sunshine of this knowledge we want to be one with Thee, living with Thee in the Divine Kingdom – radiant in Thy radiance in the Glory of God.

We know that this is impossible save by Thy prayers on our behalf. We desire earnestly and ardently to be faithful and true to Thee, as Thou art to the Blessed Perfection, pure mirrors of Thee as Thou art the pure Mirror of the Graces of God. Thy prayers will assist us to this mighty end, beloved Master; and we pray for the everlasting success of Thy Divine Mission, rejoicing that Thou art in good health, and full of love towards us.

We remain with love and deep reverence for Thee and for Thy people, and for Thy Holy Cause.

Your faithful servants[276]

Edward Hall begged Shoghi Effendi to send this supplication without changing a word. Although Shoghi Effendi did not wish his own name to be mentioned in the supplication, he graciously granted Edward's request to make him happy and agreed to send it to the Master the way it was worded.[277]

On Tuesday, 4 October 1921, Shoghi Effendi visited the premises of the Linotype Works where John Craven worked and in the evening went to John Craven's home where some of the believers and their friends had gathered. The next day 26 Bahá'ís gathered again at Mr Joseph's office and each received a silk handkerchief and carnelian stones and was anointed with attar of rose by Ḍíyá'u'lláh Aṣgharzádih. At eight o'clock in the evening everyone walked to a photographer's studio on Oldham Street to pose for a group photograph. Mr Hall wanted Shoghi Effendi to sit in the middle and hold the photograph of 'Abdu'l-Bahá but Shoghi Effendi insisted that as Mr Hall was chairman of the group, he should sit there. Mr Hall accepted.[278]

On Thursday morning, 6 October 1921 Shoghi Effendi left Manchester with Ḍíyá'u'lláh Aṣgharzádih.

16

Michaelmas Term 1921

At last the long vacation was over and Shoghi Effendi was happy to be back at university. The Michaelmas term began on 6 October 1921. The college records indicate that Shoghi Effendi participated in college various activities during the first week of term and that he used the college services for eight weeks. The last week for which there are charges against his account is the week ending 1 December 1921. The college records for the Michaelmas term 1921 show Shoghi Effendi's name in the list of students:[279]

+ Prendergast, V., J. R. D.
+ Rabbani, S., A. D. L.
+ Russell, J. A., McL.

The initials following each name correspond to the initials of each student's tutor; 'A. D. L.' was Shoghi Effendi's tutor A. D. Lindsay.

One of Shoghi Effendi's contemporaries, Paul Leroy-Beaulieu, recalls this period.

I remember him quite well although I became acquainted with him a few months only before he left. He . . . spoke both French and English fluently . . . liked to talk about the Baha'i movement. He visited me several times in my rooms which were in College, on the first floor on the left hand side of the hall, but I am sorry that I don't remember where his own rooms were located. We both attended the lectures given by T. H. Penson on economics.[280]

Shoghi Effendi was eager to take maximum advantage of the time he had at Oxford in pursuit of his main objective of perfecting his English. He carried with him a notebook in which he listed hundreds of words and typical English phrases for reference.[281]

He demanded much of himself and of his tutor. Lindsay tells of a specific encounter when Shoghi Effendi asked him for time during his dinner hour:

> I had posted my schedule . . . Shoghi Effendi came to me asking, 'What do you do between seven and half past eight?' 'Why man,' I cried, 'I dine!' 'Oh', said Shoghi Effendi with obvious disappointment, 'but must you have all that time?' I had not found so much eagerness for knowledge at Oxford. So I gave him another quarter-hour and went with less dinner. So it was – I suffered for him.[282]

One of Shoghi Effendi's contemporaries, Christopher Cox, a Balliol student of 1918–19, confirmed Shoghi Effendi's demand for Lindsay's time, an indication of his eagerness to take advantage of every minute he was in Oxford:

> The only story of him that I heard – viz his eagerness to obtain an hour a week tutorial with A. D. Lindsay, i.e. difficulty in accepting that the latter's timetable was almost full, when Lindsay showed him his timetable packed with postwar engagements, the remark that there was an hour's gap at lunchtime![283]

Another contemporary, G. W. Wrangham, a Balliol student who matriculated in 1919, relates the following:

> I remember Shoghi Effendi quite well, and in particular remember that he was then destined for his exalted position

in the Bahá'í Faith. I remember also the story that when he wanted to consult his philosophy tutor [A. D. Lindsay] on some matter of high religious or philosophical significance he was astounded to be told that he must wait until Lindsay has finished his lunch, such purely material matters as lunch ought not to have interfered with the investigation of philosophical truth.[284]

On Sunday, 9 October 1921 Shoghi Effendi took time from his work to write to the friends in Manchester. Here are excerpts from the letter he wrote from Balliol College to Edward Hall:

> My dearest Baha'i brother:
> The sweet perfume of the friends in Manchester has clung to us wherever we have gone and now that I find myself again in the cold and academic atmosphere of Oxford, my thoughts go back to the sweet hours I have spent in your midst.
> The joint supplication, one of the most potent messages ever sent to the Beloved from these shores, is now on its way to the Holy Land and as the eyes of the Master are turned towards your great city, I am confident that ere long He will respond to your joint and earnest prayers.
> I shall never fail, immersed as I am in my work, to transmit to you all the joyful tidings I may receive from anywhere regarding the Cause, and my first and last request is that the friends, one and all, may persevere to the very end in holding their regular meetings . . .[285]

In an undated letter written in Persian on Oxford Union letterhead, Shoghi Effendi stated that he had received a Tablet in honour of the believers in Manchester which contained urgent matters.[286] He translated it immediately and sent it to Mr Hall. He also stated that he was enclosing several moving prayers of the Ancient Beauty and the Master, which he had carefully translated. He mentioned that electric lights were being installed in the vicinity of the Shrine of Bahá'u'lláh by an engineer together with a few of the friends and Mírzá Luṭfu'lláh.[287]

The Tablet of the Master to the Manchester Bahá'ís was in response to their joint supplication. It was dated 18 October 1921:

> To the beloved of the Lord in the city of Manchester:
> Your letter hath been received, and the contents thereof have imparted the utmost joy and gladness. Praised be the Lord, ye have eyes that see and ears that hear. Ye beheld the Light of Truth and are accounted, even as Christ hath said, among the Chosen rather than among the Called . . . Wherefore, praise ye the Lord, that in the lamp of your hearts the Flame of Divine guidance is kindled and ye have entered the Kingdom of God. It is incumbent upon you, however, to act with utmost discretion and not rend the veil asunder, for the enemy, though he be near or afar, lieth in wait and stirreth the negligent to arise against His Holiness Bahá'u'lláh; Be ye prudent; be ye discreet.[288]

In addition to this Tablet to the believers in Manchester, the Master revealed a few individual Tablets. On 20 October 1921 the following Tablet was revealed in honour of Jacob Joseph and his brother Ibrahím. This is a paragraph from Shoghi Effendi's translation:

> O ye that stand fast and firm in the Covenant!
> The faithful servant of the Ever-Blest Beauty, Shoghi Effendi, hath written a letter, and therein hath praised you most highly, namely, that these blessed souls are true Baha'is, are verily self-sacrificing, burn brightly, even as twin candles, with the Light of Guidance, serve with heart and soul the Cause of God, succour the needy amongst the faithful, and seek fellowship with the poor.[289]

Another Tablet was revealed on the same day in honour of Samuel Heald. Here is Shoghi Effendi's translation of this Tablet:

> O son of the Kingdom of God!
> Praised be the Lord, thou hast rent asunder the veil of the Pharisees and winged thy flight unto the Kingdom of God. Thou hast accepted the Teachings of His Holiness Bahá'u'lláh and been drawn unto the Holy Spirit. In truth, thy faith is now sincere and thou hast come to know Jesus Christ better . . . .[290]

On Tuesday, 1 November 1921 Shoghi Effendi wrote to Dr Esslemont about his translation of the Hidden Words. He enclosed his version of the Ishráqát and the epistle to Queen Victoria and pointed out the immensity of the task of translation:

> My Dear Dr. Esslemont:–
> I have been of late extremely busy with my work & hope to give soon the final touch to my rendering of the Hidden Words . . . What a difficult task translation is! The more you work on it the more difficult it appears. There is simply no end to it. You can go perfecting the art ad infinitum. My only ambition however at present is to achieve a certain relative success by improving on the previous translations & if I attain this aim I am fully satisfied.[291]

On Saturday, 12 November Shoghi Effendi wrote to a Persian friend who had sent him pictures of the Manchester friends. In his letter he mentions that he had finished translating Tablets of the Master in honour of the Manchester Bahá'ís.[292]

On 22 November 1921 Shoghi Effendi wrote to John Craven from the college Junior Common Room expressing his happiness that the speedy response of the Master to the joint supplication of the friends in Manchester had so refreshed the friends and mentioning progress on his translation work:

> . . . I have been of late immersed in my work, revising many translations and have sent to Mr Hall my version of Queen Victoria's Tablet which is replete with most vital and significant world counsels, so urgently needed by this sad and disillusioned world! If you have not perused it, be sure to obtain it from Mr Hall as it is in my opinion one of the most outstanding and emphatic pronouncements of Bahá'u'lláh on world affairs . . .
>
> I am enclosing for all of you extracts, some new and some old, in the course of my readings at the Bodleian on the movement. I have also with me startling revelations on the Cause by the well-known orientalist Le Comte de Gobineau. I shall also later send you a paper on the movement which I read some time ago at one of the leading societies of Oxford.[293]

During his studies at Oxford Shoghi Effendi became familiar with a book of extreme importance, which captured his interest and left an enduring mark on the style of English that emerged in his later writings. He saw the similarity of the historical events described in the book with the decline of the social and political institutions of his time. Furthermore, he found in this book the germ of a style of English that could serve as the vehicle for the exposition of the spiritual and intellectual verities of the Faith of Bahá'u'lláh. This book, *The Decline and Fall of the Roman Empire*, Gibbon's famous work, was Shoghi Effendi's constant companion.[294]

One of Shoghi Effendi's contemporaries at Balliol, who later received the title Lord Stow Hill of Newport, describes Shoghi Effendi's fascination with this book:

> I seem to remember him walking up and down the inner quad in the grass on many occasions reading Gibbon's *Decline and Fall* as he walked, sometimes I believe aloud.

It was quite a thing to watch, and I always thought he would trip over something. However, dignity and a look of profound inspiration always seemed to be pre-served.[295]

Another Balliol student, J. M. Russell, who attended Oxford the same year as Shoghi Effendi, also refers to the walk of Shoghi Effendi in the quadrangle:

> Perhaps my clearest memories are of him walking round in the Garden Quad on summer evenings & clearly reading a small volume.[296]

In addition to Gibbon's work, Shoghi Effendi loved the style of English in the King James version of the Bible, which he read while he was at Balliol. One of his fellow students, J. C. Hill, who knew him well, has related the following:

> He read the whole of the Bible, from cover to cover in about a week. He told us he was a lover of the midnight oil.[297]

Another Balliol student, Adrian Franklin, confirms Shoghi Effendi's interest in the Bible. Franklin remembered an anecdote that circulated in the college about Shoghi Effendi:

> There was an anecdote in the college at about this time that when he came up he had never heard of the Jewish/Christian bible but, when told of it, read it Genesis to the end of New Testament in one week. I believed this at the time – I was only just 18 – but on reflection now I see the story must have been rubbish.[298]

That story was indeed inaccurate. As well as having been exposed to the Bible at the Jesuit School, Shoghi Effendi had taken four formal courses on the Bible during his freshman and sophomore years at the American University of Beirut.

Rúḥíyyih Khánum confirms that Shoghi Effendi was interested both in the Bible and in Gibbon's work:

> He was a great reader of the King James version of the Bible, and of the historians Carlyle and Gibbon, whose styles he greatly admired, particularly that of Gibbon whose *Decline and Fall of the Roman Empire* Shoghi Effendi was so fond of that I never remember his not having a volume of it near him in his room and usually with him when he travelled. There was a small Everyman's copy of part of it next to his bed when he died. It was his own pet bible of the English language and often he would read to me excerpts from it, interrupting himself with exclamations such as 'Oh what style; what a command of English; what rolling sentences; listen to this.' . . . I particularly remember one peaceful hour (so rare, alas) when we sat on a bench facing the lake on a summer afternoon in St James' Park in London and he read me Gibbon out loud. He revelled in him and throughout Shoghi Effendi's writings the influence of his style may clearly be seen, just as the biblical English is reflected in his translations of Bahá'u'lláh's Prayers, *The Hidden Words* and Tablets.[299]

17

The Last Days in England

On 29 November 1921 at 9:30 a.m. a cable reached the office
of Major Tudor-Pole in London:

> His Holiness 'Abdu'l-Bahá ascended Abhá Kingdom. Inform
> friends. Greatest Holy Leaf [300]

Major Tudor-Pole immediately notified the friends by wire.
Rúḥíyyih Khánum, in her book *The Priceless Pearl*, suggests
that Tudor-Pole must have telephoned Shoghi Effendi and
asked him to come to his office. Shoghi Effendi reached
London about noon, went to 61 St James's Street and was
shown into Tudor-Pole's private office.

> Tudor Pole [sic] was not in the room at the moment but as
> Shoghi Effendi stood there his eye was caught by the name
> of 'Abdu'l-Bahá on the open cablegram lying on the desk
> and he read it. When Tudor Pole entered the room a mo-
> ment later he found Shoghi Effendi in a state of collapse,
> dazed and bewildered by this catastrophic news. He was
> taken to the home of Miss Grand, one of the London believ-
> ers, and put to bed there for a few days. [301]

In his letter to *Star of the West* a few days later Major Tudor-
Pole wrote:

> Shoughi Rabbani and his sister will be returning to Haifa
> towards the end of the present month, and they will be

131

accompanied by Lady Blomfield, and by Ziaoullah
Asgarzade.[302]

On 29 November Dr Esslemont wrote to Shoghi Effendi with
words of comfort and inviting him to spend a few days in
Bournemouth:

> Just send me a wire . . . and I shall have a room ready for
> you . . . if I can be of any help to you in any way I shall be
> so glad. I can well imagine how heart-broken you must feel
> and how you must long to be at home and what a terrible
> blank you must feel in your life . . . Christ was closer to His
> loved ones after His ascension than before, and so I pray it
> may be with the beloved and ourselves. We must do our part
> to shoulder the responsibility of the Cause and His Spirit
> and Power will be with us and in us.[303]

On 1 December 1921 Dr Esslemont went to London. In his
diary letter to Luṭfu'lláh Ḥakím he recalls visiting Shoghi
Effendi after the passing of 'Abdu'l-Bahá:

> [I] found poor Shoghi in bed, absolutely prostrate with grief,
> at first he seemed absolutely overwhelmed by the loss,
> unable to eat, to sleep, to think, during the day. However,
> he recovered, and after tea he got up and came through to
> the drawing room, where we had a little meeting – Miss
> Grand, Lady Blomfield, Mirza Dawud, Ziaoullah and myself.
> Shoghi read and translated to us the last tablet he had
> received from the Master, and chanted for us . . .
> We gathered today at Miss Grand's again. We decided
> that Lady Blomfield would go with Shoghi and Rouhangiz
> Khanum to Haifa, as soon as the journey could be arranged.
> Ziaollah also offered to go, and bear all expenses of the
> journey, so far as necessary. That afternoon (today) Shoghi
> Effendi came to Bournemouth with me, as we thought the
> rest and change at Bournemouth while the necessary prepa-

rations were being made for the journey, would be best for him.[304]

According to Dr Esslemont, Shoghi Effendi spent the evening of 2 December through the morning of 7 December in Bournemouth. From there he wrote this significant letter to a Bahá'í student in London, reflecting the spiritual connection he had established with the Master:

> The terrible news has for some days so overwhelmed my body, my mind and my soul that I was laid for a couple of days in bed almost senseless, absent-minded and greatly agitated. Gradually His power revived me and breathed in me a confidence that I hope will henceforth guide me and inspire me in my humble work of service. The day has come, but how sudden and unexpected. The fact however that His Cause has created so many and such beautiful souls all over the world is a sure guarantee that it will live and prosper and ere long will compass the world! I am immediately starting for Haifa to receive the instruction He has left and have now made a supreme determination to dedicate my life to His service and by His aid to carry out His instructions all the days of my life . . .
>
> The stir which is now aroused in the Bahá'í world is an impetus to this Cause and will awaken every faithful soul to shoulder the responsibilities which the Master has now placed upon every one of us.
>
> The Holy Land will remain the focal centre of the Bahá'í world; a new era will now come upon it. The Master in His great vision has consolidated His work and His spirit assures me that its results will soon be made manifest.
>
> I am starting with Lady Blomfield for Haifa, and if we are delayed in London for our passage I shall then come and see you and tell you how marvellously the Master has designed His work after Him and what remarkable utterances He has pronounced with regard to the future of the Cause . . .[305]

On 5 December Edward Hall wrote to Shoghi Effendi expressing his appreciation for Shoghi Effendi's letter, which had given the friends spiritual strength during such a time of sorrow:

> Your noble letter uplifted us all and renewed our strength and determination; for if you could gather yourself together and rise above such grievous sorrow and shock, and comfort us, we, too, must do no less . . .[306]

On 8 December, Dr Esslemont wrote in his diary letter to Dr Ḥakím that Shoghi Effendi had remained in Bournemouth until the previous day when he had received a cable from the Greatest Holy Leaf urging him to return. Thereupon, Shoghi Effendi left for London to see if arrangements could be made for an earlier passage. Dr Esslemont states that Shoghi Effendi was, at times,

> . . . very sad and overcome with grief, but on the whole he kept up very bravely, and gradually, the conviction that although the bodily presence was removed, the spirit of the beloved was near, as powerful and as accessible to us as ever, seemed to revive his strength and hope. We had a small meeting of friends on Saturday evening, and the usual weekly meeting on Sunday evening, and at both he spoke with real power.[307]

Florence Pinchon, an early believer, describes the inspiring words Shoghi Effendi shared with the friends during the meeting in Bournemouth:

> Even in such distressful circumstances he sought, like the Master, to cheer and encourage us. We must not consider the smallness of our numbers. To illustrate, he related the story of how a very small, bent and wrinkled old woman asked 'Abdu'l-Bahá's permission to introduce her three sons. Whereupon three tall stalwart young men came forward and

134

stood around her. 'Behold', exclaimed the Master smilingly, to the believers present, 'from how tiny an acorn these mighty oaks have sprung.'[308]

According to Isobel Slade, Shoghi Effendi was in London on 8 December 1921. Miss Grand had invited Mrs Slade to her flat that evening. It was a solemn occasion. The friends bade farewell to Shoghi Effendi who was leaving for Haifa with Lady Blomfield to be present for the reading of 'Abdu'l-Bahá's Will. Here are Isobel Slade's recollections of that evening:

> I was particularly impressed by this very young man, whom I saw for the first time. He seemed dazed and bewildered with sadness. It was late evening and the room was very heated but he wore an overcoat. He was asked if he would not like to remove it. He replied that when he set out for England his grandfather had told him always to wear it in winter.[309]

E. C. Foster, a British believer who had met Shoghi Effendi during this period, described a meeting of Shoghi Effendi with the friends in Chelsea. The impression retained by E. C. Foster was 'that of a very grave young figure who moved quietly and with great dignity among the assembled friends'.[310]

Owing to difficulties with his passport, Shoghi Effendi could not leave as soon as he wished. He sent a cable to Haifa informing the Greatest Holy Leaf that he could not arrive until late December. 'He sailed on 16 December, accompanied by Lady Blomfield and Rouhangeze, and arrived in Haifa by train at 5.20 P.M. on 29 December from Egypt where his boat from England had docked.'[311]

A few days after his arrival in the Holy Land, Shoghi Effendi heard the provisions of the Master's Will read to him:

O my loving friends! After the passing away of this wronged one, it is incumbent upon the Aghṣán (Branches), the Afnán (Twigs) of the Sacred Lote-Tree, the Hands (pillars) of the Cause of God and the loved ones of the Abhá Beauty to turn unto Shoghi Effendi – the youthful branch branched from the two hallowed and sacred Lote-Trees and the fruit grown from the union of the two offshoots of the Tree of Holiness, – as he is the sign of God, the chosen branch, the Guardian of the Cause of God, he unto whom all the Aghṣán, the Afnán, the Hands of the Cause of God and His loved ones must turn . . .

The sacred and youthful branch, the Guardian of the Cause of God, as well as the Universal House of Justice to be universally elected and established, are both under the care and protection of the Abhá Beauty, under the shelter and unerring guidance of the Exalted One (may my life be offered up for them both). Whatsoever they decide is of God. Whoso obeyeth him not, neither obeyeth them, hath not obeyed God; whoso rebelleth against him and against them hath rebelled against God; whoso opposeth him hath opposed God; whoso contendeth with them hath contended with God; whoso disputeth with him hath disputed with God; whoso denieth him hath denied God; whoso disbelieveth in him hath disbelieved in God; whoso deviateth, separateth himself and turneth aside from him hath in truth deviated, separated himself and turned aside from God.[312]

18

The Beloved Guardian

When the Will and Testament of 'Abdu'l-Bahá was read, it became clear to all the believers that the centre of the Cause of God was Shoghi Effendi. This was the wish of the Master and the Will of God. The young Shoghi Effendi, now confronted with great responsibilities, submitted to the will of his beloved Master and accepted to take charge of the destiny of the Cause of God. This meant leaving behind the painstaking tasks of learning academic facts and perfecting his command of English in the great intellectual centre of the West. Shoghi Effendi assumed the challenges of an office that required of him a far greater degree of discipline and commitment, a field of service for which his entire past was but a divinely ordained preparation.

This chapter surveys a few highlights of the work of the Guardian during a span of 36 years, so short and yet so eventful. We who are close enough to the period of the Guardianship to have lived during Shoghi Effendi's days, to have received his stirring communications, his soul-inspiring directives, to have had the great blessing of attaining his presence – we cannot comprehend what God has wrought through His noble scion, His beloved Chosen Branch of the tree of holiness. We live in a time that is too close to his days to fully appreciate Shoghi Effendi or to gain an adequate perspective of the significance of a mission thrust upon him since time immemorial, a mission which was prophesied by the great prophet Isaiah:

And there shall come forth a rod out of the stem of Jesse, and a Branch shall grow out of his roots: And the spirit of the Lord shall rest upon him, the spirit of wisdom and understanding, the spirit of counsel and might, the spirit of knowledge and of the fear of the Lord; And shall make him of quick understanding in the fear of the Lord . . . and he shall smite the earth with the rod of his mouth, and with the breath of his lips shall he slay the wicked . . . The wolf also shall dwell with the lamb, and the leopard shall lie down with the kid; and the calf and the young lion and the fatling together; and a little child shall lead them.[313]

That little child, Shoghi Effendi, the grandson of 'Abdu'l-Bahá, the apple of His eye, was now given the mantle of the Guardianship of the Cause of God.

Retrospect

This beloved grandson of 'Abdu'l-Bahá, in whose eyes and bearing was imprinted the sign of God, had undergone the most thorough preparation for the high office he was destined to assume after the passing of the Master, a preparation that lasted all through his childhood and youth.

Although he had actively participated in student social activities at Oxford and earlier, and was remembered by his contemporaries for his eagerness, cheerful disposition, laughter and high spirits, Shoghi Effendi had experienced, throughout his student years, a series of circumstances that were difficult and often painful. During his childhood he had attended a French Jesuit school in Haifa he did not like; neither had he liked the French school he had attended in Beirut. When the Master invited him to join His entourage on the North American teaching trip, he was prevented from making that trip by Italian health officials.

During his college years, the perilous days when Palestine was involved in the world war and the life of 'Abdu'l-Bahá was in great danger, he had continued his studies away from the Master. When the war was over, he had thrown himself into the difficult, laborious and all-consuming task of translation, transcription and correspondence. In his zeal to serve the Master, he had exhausted his physical energies, requiring him to leave the land of his beloved for rest in a sanatorium in Paris. Alone in Paris, he had undergone treatment and, submissive to a strong inner urge and to the wish of the Master to pursue his further education at Oxford, he had proceeded to England to perfect his English in order to render a worthy service to the Cause of God.

At Oxford he had endured painful experiences associated with his registration and had struggled with the inner anxiety of having to learn so much in so short a time to justify his remoteness from the Holy Land. And while engaged in acquiring the knowledge he felt he needed, he was robbed of the presence of his beloved Master.

The pain this radiant youth suffered we can never comprehend. The agony of his separation from the Master during his childhood and youth, and especially immediately before the passing of the Master, none can fathom. And now that the Will and Testament of the Master was made known, Shoghi Effendi faced infinitely greater challenges.

The Task before the Guardian

Among the entire family of the Master, including his own brothers and sisters, the only person who genuinely welcomed Shoghi Effendi's appointment as the Guardian of the Cause of God and stood behind him was the Greatest Holy Leaf, the sister of 'Abdu'l-Bahá. Many felt that, owing to their seniority, they were in a position to give advice and counsel to the young Guardian. Such individuals, with petty minds and shallow faith, had forgotten the power of God's revelation and that self-serving ideas have no place in the Cause of God.

They failed to realize that the Cause of God would not be corrupted and manipulated by self-interest.

The burden Shoghi Effendi bore in having so much to study in so short a time was insignificant compared with the overwhelming responsibilities he now faced as the Guardian. Before him lay an array of difficult tasks, all to be accomplished in a short span of time.

The vast majority of the writings of Bahá'u'lláh and 'Abdu'l-Bahá, their Tablets, epistles and books, were not yet adequately translated. Bahá'u'lláh's vision that 'all that dwell on earth' would soon 'be enlisted' under the 'banners of light'[314] that welcomed Him as He set foot in 'Akká towards the Most Great Prison, was far from reality. Those holy souls whom Bahá'u'lláh had promised during His last days would be raised up to bring victory to His Cause were few in number or had not yet been born. The mighty institutions that would facilitate the coming into the Cause of the masses of humanity and which would usher in the Kingdom of God on earth were barely established. There was only a small band of believers in the East and West who, though devoted to the Cause, were unprepared to minister to the dire needs of an ailing humanity. And not least, the army of light marshalled by the Guardian faced bitter opposition from both old and new Covenant-breakers and fierce attacks by the external enemies of the Cause.

After a few months, Shoghi Effendi's physical condition declined. He needed rest. He retired to the mountains of Switzerland for two periods to recuperate and the Greatest Holy Leaf performed prescribed duties on his behalf during his absence. After his much-needed rest, the Guardian returned to the Holy Land ready to discharge his responsibilities, to fulfil the promise of God recorded in Isaiah, and to execute the divine Will for humanity.

What transpired during the period of his Guardianship is the exhilarating story of the operation of the divine Will.

140

Translation and Transliteration

While he was in England, the Guardian had already translated several of the major Tablets of Bahá'u'lláh. The Persian Hidden Words and the Tablet of Visitation were completed in the winter of 1921. The Súriy-i-Haykal, the Tablet to the Kings, the Arabic Hidden Words, the Epistle to Queen Victoria, the Tablets of Ṭarázát and Bishárát, the Epistle to Napoleon III and the Epistle to the Sháh of Iran were translated in the spring and summer of 1921.

The beloved Guardian finalized these translations and completed several others, including the Will and Testament of 'Abdu'l-Bahá, during the period that followed his assumption of the mantle of Guardianship. His translations of the writings of Bahá'u'lláh such as the *Kitáb-i-Íqán*, the *Epistle to the Son of the Wolf* and other Tablets continued one after the other.

To familiarize the Western believers with the station of the Báb and to make them aware of the early history of the Cause, the Guardian took on the task of translating parts of Nabíl's immortal narrative. But his was not merely a translation; it was a phenomenal work integrating in its footnotes the vast collection of essays, articles and letters written by travellers and orientalists of earlier generations which the beloved Guardian had assembled or discovered during his studies in the Bodleian library at Oxford.

The transliteration of the Persian and Arabic names had hitherto been inconsistent in English Bahá'í literature, such as *Star of the West*. Shoghi Effendi adopted a standardized method of transliteration which he used in *The Dawn-Breakers* to help the believers of all lands with the Persian and Arabic names of individuals and places which fill the pages of this book.

Building the Administrative Order

Concurrent with his translation work, and in conformity with the Will and Testament of 'Abdu'l-Bahá, the charter for the

World Order of Bahá'u'lláh, the Guardian directed the attention of the Bahá'í world during the years 1921 to 1937 to the principles and structure of the administrative order. He developed the constitutional structure of local and national spiritual assemblies, clarified their relationships with the community of believers and elucidated the manner of their election and operation. He emphasized that the administrative order is the channel through which the spirit of God would flow, that the Bahá'ís must be ever watchful lest 'the means supersede the end' – lest too much attention to the details of the administration deter them from its spirit.

This administrative machinery of the Cause, the necessary embryo of the future World Order of Bahá'u'lláh, thus took shape during a period of 16 years. The embryo would need to grow, develop, evolve and mature into mighty institutions that would minister to the crying needs of humanity.

The emphasis on administration and group decision-making was hard for many star teachers of the Faith to understand. A few could not accept the authority of the local spiritual assemblies and lost their faith. The majority, however, forfeited their will to the will of the institutions and stayed firm in the Covenant. They realized that the authority of the local and national assemblies was undeniable, even when such institutions were in their infancy.

Executing the Divine Teaching Plan

Referring to the Tablets of the Divine Plan, revealed by the Master to the North American Bahá'í community, as the charter for the worldwide expansion of the Cause, the Guardian initiated the first Seven Year Plan for the American Bahá'í community in 1937. He reminded this community of the distinction and primacy conferred upon it by the Master and inspired the believers to safeguard that primacy by arising to fulfil the goals of the Plan.

One year later the Guardian gave the American Bahá'í community an illuminating and momentous document, a book-length letter entitled *The Advent of Divine Justice* in which he reiterated the Will of God for that community, portrayed the role it was destined to fulfil in the spiritual transformation of the planet, praised the devoted souls from that nation who had rendered sacrificial services to the Cause, conferred upon its members the distinction of being the spiritual descendants of the Dawn-Breakers of an heroic age, explained the challenges the friends of God would have to overcome and outlined the spiritual prerequisites required for success in fulfilling their responsibility of spiritual leadership among all nations. He gave them as his special gift a soul-stirring selection from the ocean of Bahá'u'lláh's matchless utterance to inspire their hearts and comfort their souls. This immortal document, which shall be a frame of reference for America for decades to come, will continue to serve as both the diagnosis and the remedy for the social ills of this nation.

Just over two years later, at the height of World War II, the Guardian gave to the Bahá'í community yet another significant document, a second book-length letter entitled *The Promised Day is Come* in which he provided an overview of the operation of Divine Will in the social affairs of humanity. In this letter he explained that the maladies afflicting humanity must be viewed as the interposition of providence. He stated that a tempest of unexceptional violence was sweeping the face of the earth, that no one except the followers of Bahá'u-'lláh could comprehend whence it came and where it was leading. He attributed the turmoil engulfing the human race and the sufferings resulting from it as consequences of humanity's dismissal of the revelation sent by God to heal the sickness with which it was afflicted. The closing passage of the letter offers a remarkable analogy summarizing the central theme of the book and bears witness to the eloquence evident in all of the Guardian's writings:

Not ours, puny mortals that we are, to attempt, at so critical a stage in the long and checkered history of mankind, to arrive at a precise and satisfactory understanding of the steps which must successively lead a bleeding humanity, wretchedly oblivious of its God, and careless of Bahá'u'lláh, from its calvary to its ultimate resurrection. Not ours, the living witnesses of the all-subduing potency of His Faith, to question, for a moment, and however dark the misery that enshrouds the world, the ability of Bahá'u'lláh to forge, with the hammer of His Will, and through the fire of tribulation, upon the anvil of this travailing age, and in the particular shape His mind has envisioned, these scattered and mutually destructive fragments into which a perverse world has fallen, into one single unit, solid and indivisible, able to execute His design for the children of men.

Ours rather the duty, however confused the scene, however dismal the present outlook, however circumscribed the resources we dispose of, to labour serenely, confidently, and unremittingly to lend our share of assistance, in whichever way circumstances may enable us, to the operation of the forces which, as marshalled and directed by Bahá'u'lláh, are leading humanity out of the valley of misery and shame to the loftiest summits of power and glory.[315]

In this magnificent book, which will serve as a beacon of light amidst the gloom associated with trials and ordeals that will continue to engulf humanity during the dark years ahead, the Guardian explained that the sufferings meted out to the children of men serve a dual purpose as the punishment of God because of His justice and the purging of humanity because of His love. Consistent with this theme, the Guardian explained the Bahá'í view of the unfolding of dual and concurrent processes in human history – the destructive process associated with the rolling up of the old order and the constructive process identified with the birth and growth of the World Order of Bahá'u'lláh.

144

We are indeed living in an age which, if we would correctly appraise it, should be regarded as one which is witnessing a dual phenomenon. The first signalizes the death pangs of an order, effete and godless, that has stubbornly refused, despite the signs and portents of a century-old Revelation, to attune its processes to the precepts and ideals which that Heaven-sent Faith proffered it. The second proclaims the birth pangs of an Order, divine and redemptive, that will inevitably supplant the former, and within Whose administrative structure an embryonic civilization, incomparable and world-embracing, is imperceptibly maturing. The one is being rolled up, and is crashing in oppression, bloodshed, and ruin. The other opens up vistas of a justice, a unity, a peace, a culture, such as no age has ever seen. The former has spent its force, demonstrated its falsity and barrenness, lost irretrievably its opportunity, and is hurrying to its doom. The latter, virile and unconquerable, is plucking asunder its chains, and is vindicating its title to be the one refuge within which a sore-tried humanity, purged from its dross, can attain its destiny.[316]

The twin gifts of the Guardian, *The Advent of Divine Justice* and *The Promised Day is Come*, served to deepen the Bahá'ís in America and enabled them to gain a more profound sense of their mission amidst the confusion and darkness in humanity's most devastating war.

The American Bahá'í community completed the Seven Year Plan in victory and at its end celebrated the centenary, in 1944, of the declaration of the Primal Point, the Báb. On this occasion, the Guardian gave the Bahá'í community yet another gift of love, a book of unsurpassed eloquence and of significant content covering the first one hundred years of the Faith of Bahá'u'lláh. This historical account, so full of heroism, so replete with the account of the noblest demonstration of self-sacrifice the world has ever seen, so fraught with acts of barbarism and brutality toward the infant Faith of God and the inevitable culmination of such acts in the victory of that

Cause – this historical account must convince every unbiased reader of the mysterious power latent in this revelation that continues to shape the destinies of the human race. The Guardian's closing paragraph to this outstanding work, *God Passes By*, will inspire generations of believers:

> Whatever may befall this infant Faith of God in future decades or in succeeding centuries, whatever the sorrows, dangers and tribulations which the next stage in its world-wide development may engender, from whatever quarter the assaults to be launched by its present or future adversaries may be unleashed against it, however great the reverses and setbacks it may suffer, we, who have been privileged to apprehend, to the degree our finite minds can fathom, the significance of these marvellous phenomena associated with its rise and establishment, can harbour no doubt that what it has already achieved in the first hundred years of its life provides sufficient guarantee that it will continue to forge ahead, capturing loftier heights, tearing down every obstacle, opening up new horizons and winning still mightier victories until its glorious mission, stretching into the dim ranges of time that lie ahead, is totally fulfilled.[317]

The Expansion of the Cause

The expansion of the Cause continued after the first Seven Year Plan through a series of national plans in the United Kingdom, Germany, Iran and other countries. These plans, including the second Seven Year Plan for the American believers, spanned the period 1944 to 1953 and centred on the teaching of the Cause to diverse peoples in new territories and on the establishment of administrative institutions.

During the momentous years when these plans were in progress, the Guardian communicated with each national community, reminding it of its high destiny, inspiring the believers to higher levels of service and appealing in soul-

146

inspiring language to every adherent of the Cause of G\
to allow the precious opportunities of the hour to be irr\
ably lost. Here are a few examples of these appeals:

> Once again – and this time more fervently than ever before
> – I direct my plea to every single member of this strenuously
> labouring, clear-visioned, stout-hearted, spiritually endowed
> community, every man and woman, on whose individual
> efforts, resolution, self-sacrifice and perseverance the imme-
> diate destinies of the Faith of God, now traversing so crucial
> a stage in its rise and establishment primarily depends, not
> to allow, through apathy, timidity and complacency, this one
> remaining opportunity to be irretrievably lost.[318]

> Appeal to members of the community so privileged, so
> loved, so valorous, endowed with such potentialities to
> unitedly press forward however afflictive the trials their
> countrymen may yet experience . . . however onerous the
> tasks still to be accomplished, until every single obligation
> under the present Plan is honourably fulfilled . . .[319]

> The prizes within reach of this community are truly inesti-
> mable. Much will depend on the reaction of the rank and
> file of the believers to the plea now addressed to them with
> all the fervour of my soul.
> To act, and act promptly and decisively, is the need of
> the present hour and their inescapable duty. That the
> American Bahá'í community may, in this one remaining
> field, where so much is at stake, and where the needs of the
> Faith are so acute, cover itself with a glory that will outshine
> the splendour of its past exploits in the far-flung territories
> of the globe, is a prayer which I never cease to utter in my
> continual supplications to Bahá'u'lláh.[320]

As a result of these and other appeals of the Guardian and
the response of the friends, the teaching plans initiated by
him ended in victory and the message of God was spread to

the diverse elements of humanity. Local and national spiritual assemblies were established and consolidated. By 1953 the number of national spiritual assemblies had reached twelve. In this year Bahá'í communities throughout the world celebrated the centenary of the occasion in the Síyáh-Chál of Ṭihrán when Bahá'u'lláh received the first intimation of the revelation that was to flood His person and flow from His Supreme Pen for a period of nearly 40 years.

Two other events coincided with this centenary celebration. The first was the dedication of the Mother Temple of the West, the Bahá'í House of Worship in Wilmette, and the second was the announcement by the Guardian of the commencement of a ten-year long world spiritual crusade to conquer the hearts of men.

The Ten Year Crusade involved the entire Bahá'í world. It called for the cooperation of all twelve National Spiritual Assemblies as well as the believers in all lands, 'be they in active service or not, of either sex, young as well as old, rich or poor, whether veteran or newly enrolled'.[321] This Crusade would culminate in the first Bahá'í World Congress in 1963 and would celebrate the centenary of the declaration of Bahá'u'lláh in the Garden of Riḍván.

The response of the believers of the East and the West to this plan of their beloved Guardian was overwhelming. Within the short span of one year the majority of the virgin territories that constituted the pioneering goals for this plan were filled. By October 1957 the number of countries, territories and islands in which the Cause of God had penetrated had reached 254.[322]

Building the City of God

This was not all. Whilst executing the Divine Plan of the Master, the Guardian paid careful attention to the provisions of another charter of the new World Order, the Tablet of

148

Carmel in which Bahá'u'lláh refers to the City of God, prophesied in the scriptures of the past, a City that would be raised on Mount Carmel to serve as the seat of His dominion, from which the signs and evidences of His revelation, His laws and ordinances would flow unto all nations and embrace all humanity.

The Guardian meticulously raised the superstructure of the Shrine of the Báb in whose vicinity he laid to rest the sacred remains of the Greatest Holy Leaf, the sister of 'Abdu'l-Bahá. Adjacent to this holy spot, the Guardian raised monuments for Navváb, the wife of Bahá'u'lláh, the Purest Branch, Mírzá Mihdí, the brother of 'Abdu'l-Bahá, and Munírih Khánum, the wife of 'Abdu'l-Bahá. Years later he conceived the idea of a far-flung Arc embracing these resting places.

On this arc, he explained, would be raised the mighty institutions that would administer the Cause of God at its spiritual centre, thus uniting both the spiritual and administrative elements of the Faith of God on the same holy mountain. Shoghi Effendi completed the construction of the first of these structures, the Archives building, at a spot closest to the Shrine of the Báb.

The Guardian applied the same level of attention to beauty, excellence and execution of detail to all the holy places in 'Akká. He purchased, restored and beautified the holy sites where the Blessed Beauty had passed His days. This included the Mansion of Bahjí and its surroundings, the Riḍván Garden, Mazra'ih and the House of 'Abbúd.

Defending the Faith against External Attacks

As the Faith marched forward under the guidance of the Guardian, the Bahá'í community suffered repeated attacks by its enemies, particularly in Iraq, Egypt and Iran.

In Iraq the House which had been occupied by Bahá'u'lláh for nearly the entire period of His exile in that country, which had been acquired by Him and had been ordained as a place of pilgrimage, was unlawfully seized by the Shí'í community. In Egypt, the fanaticism of the local inhabitants of a village in the district of Beba precipitated shameful acts by its notary, authorized by the Ministry of Justice, who demanded that the Muslim wives of three Bahá'ís be divorced from them. The ground for such an absurd judgement was that these individuals had abandoned Islam after their legal marriages as Muslims had been registered.

In the cradle of the Faith, the persecution of the believers reached a climax towards the end of the Guardian's ministry when a premeditated campaign was launched over the air, from the pulpit and through the press, aimed at the extermination of the Bahá'í community. The disgraceful acts that emerged from this campaign were directed not only towards innocent believers but also against Bahá'í properties. The House of the Báb, ordained by Bahá'u'lláh as the most important place of pilgrimage in the cradle of the Faith, was twice desecrated, the dome of the central Bahá'í administrative headquarters was demolished and other Bahá'í administrative buildings throughout the provinces were seized and occupied.

The believers who were victims of persecution endured these difficulties with radiant acquiescence. Their Guardian, however, while deeply saddened by the events, took steps to avert the crises and the suffering by appealing to the world's highest tribunals. In each of these situations the Guardian directed the Bahá'í community to seek justice through the court systems. Hence, the Bahá'í case in Iraq was considered in successive tribunals including the court of Appeal in Iraq and finally the League of Nations. The Bahá'í case in Egypt was considered by the Appellate religious court of Beba, and won for the Faith the acknowledgement of its status as an independent religion. The Bahá'í case in Iran was brought

150

to the attention of that country's highest authorities as well as to the Secretary-General of the United Nations and the President of the Social and Economic Council.

These repeated crises abated, the Cause of God emerged triumphant and stronger through the ordeals, and the Bahá'í community established a method of confronting attacks on its members and institutions. The community demonstrated its resolve to continue its fight against persecution and injustice through the agencies of the international community.

Protecting the Covenant

Nor was this all. The Guardian, persistently and painstakingly, purified the Faith from those who broke the Covenant, who for 65 years tried unsuccessfully every possible scheme to cause a rift within the community of the Most Great Name. By the time of Shoghi Effendi's passing this band of faithless relatives of Bahá'u'lláh and 'Abdu'l-Bahá had attempted repeatedly to undermine the authority of the Guardian. By appealing to authorities, by claiming rights of inheritance, by spreading false rumours and accusations against the Head of the Faith, by seizing the key to the Shrine of Bahá'u'lláh and by continuing to occupy the Mansion of Bahjí, these misguided opponents of the Faith of God inflicted severe blows to the body of the Cause and saddened the heart of the Guardian. Yet, despite temporary setbacks, the Cause of God continued its onward march, purified and stronger than before, along its destined course.

By the time of the Guardian's passing, all the holy grounds legally belonged to the Bahá'í community and were permanently secured from the influence of the Covenant-breakers. The Shrine of Bahá'u'lláh and the Mansion of Bahjí had been returned, restored and beautified. The buildings adjacent to the Mansion were acquired and demolished. The gardens surrounding the most sacred spot on earth, the Ḥaram-i-

Aqdas, the Qiblih of the people of Bahá, were designed and filled with beautiful plants and flowers under the Guardian's close supervision.

Preparing the Transition to the Future

Finally, the Guardian, faithful to the provisions of the Will and Testament of 'Abdu'l-Bahá, the charter of the World Order of Bahá'u'lláh, selected from among the faithful a number of dedicated believers and elevated them to the rank of 'Hand of the Cause of God'. These souls responded with devotion and loyalty to the call of their beloved, ready to sacrifice their all at his command. The Guardian inspired, nurtured, trained and developed this small band of heroic and self-sacrificing servants, who numbered 27 at the time of his passing, and entrusted them with the stewardship of the Cause of God, confident that they would be capable of keeping the ship of the Cause on its predestined course and of steering it towards its ultimate destination. Shoghi Effendi announced the appointment of the last contingent of Hands of the Cause just before his passing:

> So marvellous a progress, embracing so vast a field, achieved in so short a time, by so small a band of heroic souls, well deserves, at this juncture in the evolution of a decade-long Crusade, to be signalized by, and indeed necessitates, the announcement of yet another step in the progressive unfoldment of one of the cardinal and pivotal institutions ordained by Bahá'u'lláh, and confirmed in the Will and Testament of 'Abdu'l-Bahá, involving the designation of yet another contingent of the Hands of the Cause of God, raising thereby to thrice nine the total number of the Chief Stewards of Bahá'u'lláh's embryonic World Commonwealth, who have been invested by the unerring Pen of the Centre of His Covenant with the dual function of guarding over the security, and of insuring the propagation, of His Father's Faith.[323]

It was this body of steadfast and dedicated Hands of the Cause who, though heart-broken and bewildered by the passing of their beloved leader, stood firm at the hour of trial and refused, except in a single case[324] to act in any manner that would inflict the slightest harm to the unity of the Faith of God. Theirs was the supreme challenge of preserving the integrity of the Cause whose custodianship had been entrusted to them, a challenge which they met superbly. It was they who handed the reins of authority of a Bahá'í world community undivided and undeterred to that infallible institution, the Universal House of Justice, in 1963.

A Mansion of Love

Just before the mid-point of the Ten Year Plan, on the autumn day of 4 November 1957, the Blessed Beauty called Shoghi Effendi to His other dominions, confident that the ark of salvation, the ship of the Cause of God would continue its course toward its ultimate destiny. The Guardian, having finished his work on this earthly plane, ascended to the realms beyond, leaving an army of bereaved, yet dedicated and determined souls to complete the execution of the processes which he had set in motion, processes whose unfoldment would engage hundreds of future generations.

The Guardian's Legacy

The writings of the Faith had been translated by Shoghi Effendi into the most perfect English, conveying accurately and forcefully the revelation of God to the Western world. Future translations would follow his standard.

The salient features of the Faith's history, laws and administration had been delineated and fully explained in a language and in a style comprehensible to the believers of both the East and the West. A standardized transliteration

153

of the names associated with the heroes and heroines of the Apostolic Age and the sacred spots associated with that age had been adopted and references to such names in later Bahá'í literature would follow the same system.

The principles of the administrative order of the Faith, rooted in the writings of Bahá'u'lláh and in the Will and Testament of 'Abdu'l-Bahá had been fully explained to the believers. The machinery of the administration had been reared by Shoghi Effendi and used to accomplish seemingly impossible tasks. Now that he was gone, this administrative order would continue to grow to maturity following the standard he had set, without the slightest deviation from principle.

The pattern for executing the Divine Plan of the Master for the conquest of the hearts of men had been established and incremental plans to realize the goals of that Plan had been undertaken. Future plans would follow this example.

The standard for the buildings on Mount Carmel, mighty institutions that would serve as the beacon of light in a dark and confused world, had been established. The gardens surrounding those buildings had been laid out, the style of architecture that would express the spirit of those buildings had been defined through the first structure, the Archives building. The remaining edifices of the arc would be constructed in the same style.

The claims of the Covenant-breakers to Bahá'í properties had been greatly reduced and most rights transferred to the institutions of the Faith. The influence of the Covenant-breakers was overshadowed by the onward march of the Cause of God and the community purified from their poison. The responses to those who would attempt to violate the Covenant in the future would follow the same standard.

Looking back at the life and work of Shoghi Effendi, we see how marvellous was his handiwork, how beautiful his design and how perfect the sequence of events that transpired after his assumption of the mantle of Guardianship. The longing of his heart, so often expressed to the friends while he was a student at Oxford – that he properly equip himself for service to the Cause – had been fulfilled.

Shoghi Effendi, that young Oxford student who became the Guardian of the Cause of God, left a legacy which will astound generations of humanity. No words of ours can adequately convey the admiration, love, gratitude and devotion which are his due. The words that befit him best are his own, written on the occasion of the passing of the Greatest Holy Leaf:

> Whatever betide us, however distressing the vicissitudes which the nascent Faith of God may yet experience, we pledge ourselves, before the mercy-seat of thy glorious Father, to hand on, unimpaired and undivided, to generations yet unborn, the glory of that tradition of which thou hast been its most brilliant exemplar.
>
> In the innermost recesses of our hearts . . . we have reared for thee a shining mansion that the hand of time can never undermine, a shrine which shall frame eternally the matchless beauty of thy countenance, an altar whereon the fire of thy consuming love shall burn forever.[325]

Bibliography

Bahá'í World, The. vols. 1–12, 1925–54. rpt. Wilmette, Ill.: Bahá'í Publishing Trust, 1980.

— vol. 13. Haifa: The Universal House of Justice, 1970.

— vol. 14. Haifa: The Universal House of Justice, 1974.

— vol. 15. Haifa: Bahá'í World Centre, 1976.

Balyuzi, H. M. *'Abdu'l-Bahá*. Oxford: George Ronald, 1971.

Blomfield, Lady [Sara Louise]. *The Chosen Highway*. Wilmette, Ill.: Bahá'í Publishing Trust, 1967.

Carless Davis, H. W. *A History of Balliol College*. Oxford: A. R. Mowbray & Co., 1963.

Commonwealth Universities Yearbook, vol. 3, 1994.

Dictionary of National Biography, 1901–1960. Oxford University Press, 1971.

Gail, Marzieh. *Arches of the Years*. Oxford: George Ronald, 1991.

Hall, E. T. *Bahá'í Dawn – Early Days of the Bahá'í Faith in Manchester*. Manchester: Bahá'í Assembly, 1925.

Jones, John. *Balliol College Oxford, A Brief History and Guide*. Abingdon: Leach's, 1993.

Momen, Moojan. *Dr. John Ebenezer Esslemont*. London: Bahá'í Publishing Trust, 1975.

Nabíl-i-A'zam. *The Dawn-Breakers: Nabíl's Narrative of the Early Days of the Bahá'í Revelation*. Wilmette, Ill.: Bahá'í Publishing Trust, 1970.

Penrose, Stephen B. L. *That They May Have Life*. Princeton University Press, 1941.

Rabbaní, Rúḥíyyih. *The Priceless Pearl*. London: Bahá'í Publishing Trust, 1969.

Shoghi Effendi. *Bahá'í Administration*. Wilmette, Ill.: Bahá'í Publishing Trust, 1968.

— *Citadel of Faith: Messages to America 1947–1957*. Wilmette, Ill.: Bahá'í Publishing Trust, 1965.

— *God Passes By*. Wilmette, Ill.: Bahá'í Publishing Trust, rev. edn. 1974.

— *Messages to the Bahá'í World*. Wilmette, Ill.: Bahá'í Publishing Trust, 1971.

— *The Promised Day is Come*. Wilmette, Ill.: Bahá'í Publishing Trust, rev. edn. 1980.

Star of the West. Rpt. Oxford: George Ronald, 1984.

Weinberg, Robert. *Ethel Jenner Rosenberg: The Life and Times of England's Outstanding Bahá'í Pioneer Worker*. Oxford: George Ronald, 1995.

Whitehead, O. Z. *Some Bahá'ís to Remember*. Oxford: George Ronald, 1983.

Who's Who, 1920.

Yazdi, Ali. M. *Blessings Beyond Measure: Recollections of 'Abdu'l-Bahá and Shoghi Effendi.* Wilmette, Ill.: Bahá'í Publishing Trust, 1988.

Notes and References

1. Tablet of 'Abdu'l-Bahá about Shoghi Effendi, in Rabbaní, *Priceless Pearl*, p. 2.
2. Letter from the Universal House of Justice to the author, 21 July 1967.
3. Letters from St Catherine's College and Balliol College to the author, 1 September 1993 and 25 August 1993.
4. Rabbaní, *Priceless Pearl*, p. 4.
5. The date mentioned in *Priceless Pearl* is the most reliable date as it appears to be consistent with several instances when Shoghi Effendi had to declare his age, although not all. The early registration forms at the Syrian Protestant College did not require a birth date, only the age of the student; it was only in 1917 that the registration forms began to require a birth date. This may be because a person's birthday was not given the great emphasis it is in the West and many people born in the latter part of the 19th century and early part of the 20th century did not have any idea when they were born. My father was among them. He used to tell his family that the time of his birth was recorded in a volume that contained the sacred writings of the Faith but that the book was lost. He chose 1 January 1904 as a close estimate because it was easy to remember.
6. Nabíl-i-A'ẓam, *Dawn-Breakers*, genealogy chart.
7. Quoted in Rabbaní, *Priceless Pearl*, p. 5.
8. ibid. p. 4.
9. ibid. p. 17.
10. ibid. p. 9.
11. ibid.
12. According to Rabbaní, *Priceless Pearl*, pp. 15–17, this school was located in Haifa.
13. Interview with Dr Mo'ayyid, 1970.

14. Rabbaní, *Priceless Pearl*, p. 17.
15. ibid. p. 13.
16. Yazdi, *Blessings Beyond Measure*, p. 50.
17. Rabbaní, *Priceless Pearl*, p. 19.
18. Yazdi, *Blessings Beyond Measure*, pp. 51–3.
19. Rabbaní, *Priceless Pearl*, pp. 19–20.
20. Interview with Dr Mo'ayyid, 1970.
21. Rabbaní, *Priceless Pearl*, pp. 20, 24.
22. Quoted in ibid. p. 21.
23. ibid.
24. Rabbaní, *Priceless Pearl*, p. 17.
25. Interview with Dr Mo'ayyid, 1970.
26. College records, American University of Beirut, sent to the author by the university registrar.
27. This section on the history and background of the Syrian Protestant College is taken from Penrose, *That They May Have Life*.
28. ibid. p. 2.
29. ibid. pp. 8–10.
30. ibid. p. 29.
31. Rabbaní, *Priceless Pearl*, p. 21.
32. ibid. p. 22.
33. Transcripts of Shoghi Effendi, sent to the author by the American University of Beirut.
34. College Records, American University of Beirut, sent to the author by the university registrar.
35. ibid.
36. Quoted in *Bahá'í World*, vol. 13, p. 67.
37. ibid.
38. Penrose, *That They May Have Life*, p. 150.
39. ibid. p. 151.
40. ibid. p. 153.
41. Transcripts of Shoghi Effendi, sent to the author by the American University of Beirut.
42. College Records, American University of Beirut, sent to the author by the university registrar.
43. *Star of the West*, vol. 9, no. 9, p. 99.
44. Interview with Dr Mo'ayyid, 1970.

45. Yazdi, *Blessings Beyond Measure*, pp. 55–7.
46. Transcripts of Shoghi Effendi, sent to the author by the American University of Beirut.
47. ibid.
48. College Records, American University of Beirut, sent to the author by the university registrar.
49. Penrose, *That They May Have Life*, p. 159.
50. ibid. p. 162.
51. Transcripts of Shoghi Effendi, sent to the author by the American University of Beirut.
52. College Records, American University of Beirut, sent to the author by the university registrar.
53. Rabbaní, *Priceless Pearl*, pp. 25–6.
54. Balyuzi, *'Abdu'l-Bahá*, p. 429.
55. Rabbaní, *Priceless Pearl*, p. 23.
56. See, for example, *Bahá'í Year Book*, vol. 1, pp. 12–15.
57. *Bahá'í World*, vol. 15, p. 431.
58. Momen, *Esslemont*, p. 10.
59. Archives of the National Spiritual Assembly of the Bahá'ís of the United Kingdom. See also *Star of the West*, vol. 9, no. 17, p. 195.
60. *Star of the West*, vol. 10, no. 1, pp. 8–10.
61. ibid. vol. 9, no. 17, p. 196.
62. ibid. vol. 10, no. 1, p. 3.
63. ibid. vol. 9, no. 17, p. 197.
64. ibid. pp. 194–6.
65. Yazdi, *Blessings Beyond Measure*, p. 62.
66. *Star of the West*. vol. 10, no. 2, pp. 17–19 and vol. 10, no. 1, pp. 7–12.
67. ibid. vol. 10, no. 1, p. 11.
68. ibid. vol. 10, no. 1, pp. 3, 9, 13.
69. Archives of the National Spiritual Assembly of the Bahá'ís of the United Kingdom.
70. *Star of the West*, vol. 9, no. 19, p. 223; vol. 10, no. 1, pp. 8, 13–14; vol. 10, no. 2, pp. 28–9, 338–40; vol. 10, no. 19, p. 340.
71. ibid. vol. 10, no. 3, p. 39.

72. ibid. vol. 10, no. 1, pp. 12–13; vol. 10, no. 2, pp. 29–32; vol. 10, no. 3, pp. 42–3; vol. 10, no. 7, p. 143.
73. ibid. vol. 10, no. 2, p. 31.
74. ibid. vol. 10, no. 3, pp. 40–1, 43; vol. 10, no. 4, pp. 76–8; vol. 10, no. 7, pp. 136–7, 144.
75. ibid. vol. 9, no. 19, p. 220.
76. ibid. vol. 10, no. 1, pp. 10–11; vol. 10, no. 3, pp. 41–2; vol. 10, no. 4, pp. 79–80; vol. 10, no. 6, p. 110; vol. 10, no. 17, p. 316.
77. ibid. vol. 10, no. 2, p. 23.
78. For example, Blomfield, *Chosen Highway*.
79. *Star of the West*, vol. 10, no. 11, p. 217.
80. ibid. pp. 217–18.
81. Sometime married to Ahmad Sohrab, whom she divorced when he broke the Covenant.
82. *Star of the West*, vol. 10, no. 11, pp. 218–20.
83. ibid. p. 220.
84. ibid. vol. 11, no. 3, pp. 48–9.
85. ibid. pp. 49–50.
86. ibid. pp. 50–1.
87. ibid. p. 51.
88. ibid. p. 52.
89. ibid. pp. 52–3.
90. ibid. pp. 53–4.
91. ibid. vol. 10, no. 5, p. 96; vol. 10, no. 9, p. 185.
92. ibid. vol. 10, no. 5, p. 96.
93. ibid. vol. 10, no. 3, p. 36.
94. ibid. pp. 43–4.
95. ibid. p 44.
96. ibid. vol. 10, no. 4, p. 73.
97. ibid. vol. 10, no. 7, p. 143; vol. 10, no. 9, pp. 184–5.
98. ibid. vol. 10, no. 9, p. 184.
99. ibid. vol. 10, no. 6, p. 109.
100. ibid. vol. 10, no. 11, p. 221; vol. 10, no. 19, pp. 340–1.
101. ibid. vol. 10, no. 11, p. 221.
102. ibid. vol. 10, no. 8, p. 153.
103. ibid. vol. 10, no. 6, pp. 104–6.
104. ibid. vol. 5, no. 5, pp. 94–5.

105. ibid. vol. 10, no. 7, pp. 135–6.
106. ibid. vol. 10, no. 8, pp. 156–64.
107. Archives of the National Spiritual Assembly of the Bahá'ís of the United Kingdom.
108. *Star of the West*, vol. 10, no. 8, p. 155.
109. ibid. p. 168.
110. ibid. vol. 11, no. 1, pp. 15–19.
111. ibid. vol. 10, no. 8, p. 165.
112. Archives of the National Spiritual Assembly of the Bahá'ís of the United Kingdom.
113. *Star of the West*, vol. 10, no. 12, p. 233; vol. 10, no. 14, p. 267.
114. Archives of the National Spiritual Assembly of the Bahá'ís of the United Kingdom.
115. *Star of the West*, vol. 10, no. 17, pp. 317–18.
116. ibid. vol. 10, no. 12, pp. 233–4, 236; vol. 10, no. 14, pp. 267–8, 272; vol. 10, no. 17, pp. 318–19.
117. ibid. vol. 10, no. 12, pp. 234–6; vol. 10, no. 13, pp. 250–1; vol. 10, no. 14, p. 268; vol. 11, no. 10, pp. 159–64, 166–8; vol. 11, no. 16, p. 276.
118. ibid. vol. 10, no. 13, p. 246; vol. 10, no. 14, pp. 268–70; vol. 10, no. 17, pp. 319–20; vol. 10, no. 18, pp. 329–30; vol. 11, no. 3, p. 54; vol. 11, no. 4, p. 76; vol. 11, no. 6, p. 104.
119. ibid. vol. 10, no. 13, p. 245; vol. 10, no. 19, pp. 339–40.
120. ibid. vol. 10, no. 13, p. 246; vol. 11, no. 5, p. 92; vol. 11, no. 10, p. 165; vol. 11, no. 14, pp. 240–3.
121. ibid. vol. 10, no. 17, p. 319; vol. 11, no. 16, pp. 277–8.
122. ibid. vol. 10, no. 14, pp. 270–1; vol. 10, no. 19, p. 342; vol. 11, no. 10, pp. 165–6.
123. ibid. vol. 10, no. 13, pp. 247–9.
124. ibid. vol. 10, no. 13, pp. 246–7.
125. ibid. vol. 11, no. 16, p. 276.
126. ibid. vol. 10, no. 12, p. 236.
127. ibid. vol. 10, no. 18, pp. 329–30.
128. The original letters are to be found in the Archives of the National Spiritual Assembly of the Bahá'ís of the United Kingdom. These summaries of the diary letters of Shoghi

163

Effendi convey the author's understanding of the text of the letters. The reader should regard the summaries as having the same authenticity as pilgrims' notes. For a more accurate understanding of the content of the diary letters, the reader is encouraged to refer to the originals.

129. Yazdi, *Blessings Beyond Measure*, p. 65.
130. *Star of the West*, vol. 11, no. 10, pp. 167–8; vol. 11, no. 13, p. 232.
131. ibid. vol. 10, no. 19, p. 342; vol. 11, no. 16, pp. 278–80.
132. ibid. vol. 11, no. 10, p. 166.
133. Momen, *Esslemont*, pp. 19–20.
134. Yazdi, *Blessings Beyond Measure*, p. 70.
135. ibid. p. 71.
136. *Star of the West*, vol. 11, no. 8, pp. 133–4.
137. ibid. vol. 11, no. 15, pp. 259–60; vol. 11, no. 18, pp. 306–8.
138. Momen, *Esslemont*, p. 20.
139. Rabbaní, *Priceless Pearl*, p. 32.
140. Letter from the collection of Mr Z. Khadem.
141. *Bahá'í World*, vol. 14, p. 352. See also Gail, *Arches of the Years*, pp. 179–86.
142. Letter from the collection of Mr Z. Khadem.
143. Yazdi, *Blessings Beyond Measure*, pp. 72–3.
144. Letter from the collection of Mr Z. Khadem.
145. ibid.
146. Letter from St Catherine's College Office.
147. Archives of the National Spiritual Assembly of the Bahá'ís of the United Kingdom.
148. Yazdi, *Blessings Beyond Measure*, pp. 74–5.
149. ibid. p. 74.
150. Archives of the National Spiritual Assembly of the Bahá'ís of the United Kingdom.
151. Letter from the collection of Mr Z. Khadem.
152. ibid.
153. Rabbaní, *Priceless Pearl*, pp. 11–13.
154. After Lord Lamington's death, Lady Lamington sent to the British National Spiritual Assembly the ring given to her husband by the Master.

155. Letter from Shoghi Effendi, Archives of the National Spiritual Assembly of the Bahá'ís of the United Kingdom.
156. Archives of the National Spiritual Assembly of the Bahá'ís of the United Kingdom.
157. *Who's Who*, 1920.
158. Balyuzi, *'Abdu'l-Bahá*, p. 156.
159. Weinberg, *Ethel Rosenberg*, p. 173.
160. Letter in the Archives of the National Spiritual Assembly of the Bahá'ís of the United Kingdom. See also ibid. pp. 173–4.
161. Letter in the Archives of the National Spiritual Assembly of the Bahá'ís of the United Kingdom.
162. This section on the history and background of Balliol College is taken from Davis, *History of Balliol College*.
163. Davis, *History of Balliol College*, p. 2.
164. ibid. pp. 6–9.
165. Letter from Shoghi Effendi in Persian in the Archives of the National Spiritual Assembly of the Bahá'ís of the United Kingdom.
166. *Balliol College Oxford, A Brief History and Guide*, p. 8.
167. Davis, *History of Balliol College*, p. 239.
168. ibid. p. 244.
169. *Dictionary of National Biography*, 1901–1960. See also Davis, *History of Balliol College*, pp. 261–7. In 1922 Lindsay left Balliol to accept the post of Professor of moral philosophy at Glasgow but returned in 1924 as the Master of the college upon the death of A. L. Smith. In 1935 he was appointed Vice-Chancellor of the University of Oxford.
170. Davis, *History of Balliol College*, pp. 260–1.
171. *Who's Who*, 1920.
172. ibid.
173. Letter in the Archives of the National Spiritual Assembly of the Bahá'ís of the United Kingdom. See also, Rabbaní, *Priceless Pearl*, pp. 32–3.
174. Quoted in Rabbaní, *Priceless Pearl*, p. 33.
175. Letter in the Archives of the National Spiritual Assembly of the Bahá'ís of the United Kingdom.
176. Balyuzi, *'Abdu'l-Bahá*, p. 356.

177. Esslemont letters in the Archives of the National Spiritual Assembly of the Bahá'ís of the United Kingdom.
178. Letter in the Archives of the National Spiritual Assembly of the Bahá'ís of the United Kingdom.
179. Letter from A. D. Lindsay to J. B. Baker, collected by author from St Catherine's College.
180. Located in the centre of the city of Oxford.
181. A history of St Catherine's College.
182. *Commonwealth Universities Yearbook*, 1994, vol. 3.
183. Copy of letter in author's collection.
184. St Catherine's College records.
185. Ali Yazdi had been sent by the Master to Germany to prepare for his further education in the United States. The sum given to him by the Master was dwindling and Ali was concerned about having enough to make the trip.
186. Yazdi, *Blessings Beyond Measure*, pp. 80–2.
187. *Balliol College Oxford, A Brief History and Guide*, pp. 33–4.
188. This is based on the experience of the author during the academic years 1964–8. The description of life at Oxford in this chapter reflects conditions at the university in 1964, which were not very different from those in 1920.
189. ibid.
190. ibid.
191. ibid.
192. ibid.
193. Adapted from Rabbaní, *Priceless Pearl*, p. 36.
194. Letter from Dr Esslemont to Luṭfu'lláh Ḥakím, Archives of the National Spiritual Assembly of the Bahá'ís of the United Kingdom.
195. Quoted in Rabbaní, *Priceless Pearl*, p. 37.
196. College Records, St Catherine's College.
197. A form of greeting performed by Persian men.
198. Yazdi, *Blessings Beyond Measure*, pp. 82–3.
199. ibid. p. 83.
200. ibid. p. 85.
201. ibid. pp. 85–6.
202. Letter in the Archives of the National Spiritual Assembly of the Bahá'ís of the United Kingdom.

203. Inter-college correspondence, St Catherine's College.
204. Letter from Lindsay to Baker, St Catherine's College.
205. Letter from Baker to Lindsay, St Catherine's College.
206. ibid.
207. Letter from Lindsay to Bailey, Balliol College.
208. Balliol College records.
209. *Balliol College Oxford, A Brief History and Guide*, pp. 33–9.
210. Bursary files, Balliol College.
211. Letter from A. Boyce Gibson to the author, 3 May 1969.
212. Bursary files, Balliol College.
213. Quoted in Rabbaní, *Priceless Pearl*, p. 37.
214. Letter from Shoghi Effendi in Persian in the Archives of the National Spiritual Assembly of the Bahá'ís of the United Kingdom. As no official translation of this letter exists, the summary presented here conveys the author's understanding of the text of the letter and should be regarded with the same authenticity as pilgrims' notes. For a more accurate understanding of the content of the letter, the reader is encouraged to refer to the original text.
215. Dr J. Estlin Carpenter was the Principal of Manchester College when the Master visited there in 1913. He presided at the meeting where 'Abdu'l-Bahá spoke and paid an eloquent tribute to His work and the message He was delivering to the western world. Further, in his book, *Comparative Religion*, he refers to the Bahá'í Faith and asks, '. . . has Persia, in the midst of her miseries, given birth to a religion which will go around the world?' Quoted in Balyuzi, *'Abdu'l-Bahá*, p. 354.
216. Letter in the Archives of the National Spiritual Assembly of the Bahá'ís of the United Kingdom.
217. Letter from Dr Esslemont to Dr Luṭfu'lláh Ḥakím, Archives of the National Spiritual Assembly of the Bahá'ís of the United Kingdom.
218. Letter of Shoghi Effendi to Dr Esslemont in the Archives of the National Spiritual Assembly of the Bahá'ís of the United Kingdom.
219. College records, Balliol College.

220. Letter from Dr Esslemont to Luṭfu'lláh Ḥakím in the Archives of the National Spiritual Assembly of the Bahá'ís of the United Kingdom.
221. Letter from J. C. Hill to the author, 29 May 1969.
222. Letter from Geoffrey Meade to the author, 18 April 1969.
223. Letter from Adrian Franklin to the author, 17 April 1969.
224. Letter from G. Raleigh to the author, 23 June 1969.
225. Letter from J. C. Dwyer to the author, 24 May 1969.
226. *Bahá'í World,* vol. 13, pp. 881–2.
227. Letter from Shoghi Effendi in Persian in the Archives of the National Spiritual Assembly of the Bahá'ís of the United Kingdom. As no official translation of this letter exists, the summary presented here conveys the author's understanding of the text and should be regarded with the same authenticity as pilgrims' notes. For a more accurate understanding of the content of the letter, the reader is encouraged to refer to the original.
228. Archives of the National Spiritual Assembly of the Bahá'ís of the United Kingdom.
229. Letter from Shoghi Effendi in Persian in the Archives of the National Spiritual Assembly of the Bahá'ís of the United Kingdom. As no official translation of this letter exists, the summary presented here conveys the author's understanding of the text and should be regarded with the same authenticity as pilgrims' notes. For a more accurate understanding of the content of the letter, the reader is encouraged to refer to the original.
230. Letter from Shoghi Effendi in Persian in the Archives of the National Spiritual Assembly of the Bahá'ís of the United Kingdom. As no official translation of this letter exists, the summary presented in this chapter, conveying the author's understanding of the text of the letter, should be regarded with the same authenticity as pilgrims' notes. For a more accurate understanding of the content of the letter, the reader is encouraged to refer to the original text.
231. Bursary files, Balliol College.
232. Letter in the Archives of the National Spiritual Assembly of the Bahá'ís of the United Kingdom.

ENCES

233. Letter from Shoghi Effendi in Persian in the Archives of the National Spiritual Assembly of the Bahá'ís of the United Kingdom. As no official translation of this letter exists, the summary presented here conveys the author's understanding of the text and should be regarded with the same authenticity as pilgrims' notes. For a more accurate understanding of the content of the letter, the reader is encouraged to refer to the original.
234. Letter from G. C. Greer to the author, 23 June 1969.
235. Letter from Lord Stow Hill of Newport, Mr Soskice, to the author, 19 May 1969.
236. Letter from A. W. Davis to the author, 21 April 1969.
237. Letter from B. H. Bevan-Petman to the author, 18 May 1969.
238. Letter from Geoffrey Meade to the author, 18 April 1969.
239. Persian shoes made with cloth.
240. Letter from J. C. Hill to the author.
241. Letter from S. P. Streuve to the author, 27 May 1969.
242. *Bahá'í News*, no. 121, p. 11.
243. ibid.
244. Bahá'u'lláh, *Prayers and Meditations*, pp. 288–93.
245. Letter from William Elliot to the author, 15 July 1969.
246. Quoted in Rabbaní, *Priceless Pearl*, p. 34.
247. ibid.
248. Letter from Shoghi Effendi in Persian in the Archives of the National Spiritual Assembly of the Bahá'ís of the United Kingdom. As no official translation of this letter exists, the summary presented in this chapter, conveying the author's understanding of the text of the letter, should be regarded with the same authenticity as pilgrims' notes. For a more accurate understanding of the content of the letter, the reader is encouraged to refer to the original text.
249. Letter from Edna True to the author, 23 April 1969.
250. Letter from L. Forbes-Ritte to the author, 1969.
251. Letter from G. E. Lavin to the author, 1969.
252. Letter of Dr Esslemont to Luṭfu'lláh Ḥakím in the Archives of the National Spiritual Assembly of the Bahá'ís of the United Kingdom.

169

253. Letter in the Archives of the National Spiritual Assembly of the Bahá'ís of the United Kingdom.
254. Letter from Shoghi Effendi in Persian in the Archives of the National Spiritual Assembly of the Bahá'ís of the United Kingdom. As no official translation of this letter exists, the summary presented here conveys the author's understanding of the text and should be regarded with the same authenticity as pilgrims' notes. For a more accurate understanding of the content of the letter, the reader is encouraged to refer to the original.
255. Letter in the Archives of the National Spiritual Assembly of the Bahá'ís of the United Kingdom.
256. Letter from Shoghi Effendi in Persian in the Archives of the National Spiritual Assembly of the Bahá'ís of the United Kingdom. As no official translation of this letter exists, the summary presented here conveys the author's understanding of the text and should be regarded with the same authenticity as pilgrims' notes. For a more accurate understanding of the content of the letter, the reader is encouraged to refer to the original.
257. Letter in the Archives of the National Spiritual Assembly of the Bahá'ís of the United Kingdom.
258. Whitehead, *Some Bahá'ís to Remember*, p. 55.
259. Letter from Shoghi Effendi in Persian in the Archives of the National Spiritual Assembly of the Bahá'ís of the United Kingdom. As no official translation of this letter exists, the summary presented here conveys the author's understanding of the text and should be regarded with the same authenticity as pilgrims' notes. For a more accurate understanding of the content of the letter, the reader is encouraged to refer to the original.
260. ibid.
261. ibid.
262. Letter in the Archives of the National Spiritual Assembly of the Bahá'ís of the United Kingdom.
263. Whitehead, *Some Bahá'ís to Remember*, p. 57.
264. ibid. pp. 31–4.
265. ibid. p. 53.

266. Hall, *Bahá'í Dawn*.
267. ibid. pp. 22–3.
268. Lucy Hall's autograph book.
269. Hall, *Bahá'í Dawn*, p. 23.
270. Letter from Lucy Hall to the author, 7 July 1969.
271. ibid.
272. Hall, *Bahá'í Dawn*.
273. Letter from Lucy Hall to the author, 7 July 1969.
274. ibid.
275. Hall, *Bahá'í Dawn*, p. 24.
276. Whitehead, *Some Bahá'ís to Remember*, pp. 59–60.
277. Letter from Lucy Hall to the author, 7 July 1969.
278. ibid.
279. Balliol College records.
280. Letter from Paul Leroy-Beaulieu to the author, 1969.
281. Rabbaní, *Priceless Pearl*, p. 37.
282. Quoted in ibid. p. 35.
283. Letter from Christopher W. M. Cox to the author, 1969.
284. Letter from G. W. Wrangham to the author, 1969.
285. Letter from Shoghi Effendi to E. T. Hall, Lucy Hall's papers.
286. Letter from Shoghi Effendi in Persian in the Archives of the National Spiritual Assembly of the Bahá'ís of the United Kingdom. As no official translation of this letter exists, the summary presented here conveys the author's understanding of the text of the letter and should be regarded with the same authenticity as pilgrims' notes. For a more accurate understanding of the content of the letter, the reader is encouraged to refer to the original text.
287. Letter from Shoghi Effendi in Persian in the Archives of the National Spiritual Assembly of the Bahá'ís of the United Kingdom. As no official translation of this letter exists, the summary presented in this chapter, conveying the author's understanding of the text of the letter, should be regarded with the same authenticity as pilgrims' notes. For a more accurate understanding of the content of the letter, the reader is encouraged to refer to the original text.
288. Hall, *Bahá'í Dawn*, p. 27.

289. ibid.
290. Quoted in Whitehead, *Some Bahá'ís to Remember*, p. 63.
291. Letter in the Archives of the National Spiritual Assembly of the Bahá'ís of the United Kingdom.
292. Letter from Shoghi Effendi in Persian in the Archives of the National Spiritual Assembly of the Bahá'ís of the United Kingdom. As no official translation of this letter exists, the summary presented here conveys the author's understanding of the text of the letter and should be regarded with the same authenticity as pilgrims' notes. For a more accurate understanding of the content of the letter, the reader is encouraged to refer to the original text.
293. Letter from Shoghi Effendi to John Craven in the Archives of the National Spiritual Assembly of the Bahá'ís of the United Kingdom.
294. Rabbaní, *Priceless Pearl*, pp. 37–8.
295. Letter from Lord Stow Hill of Newport, Mr Soskice, to the author, 11 July 1966.
296. Letter from J. M. Russell to the author, 1969.
297. Letter from J. C. Hill to the author, 29 May 1969.
298. Letter from Adrian Franklin to the author, 1969.
299. Rabbaní, *Priceless Pearl*, pp. 37–8.
300. Quoted in Rabbaní, *Priceless Pearl*, p. 39.
301. ibid.
302. *Star of the West*, vol. 12, no. 16, p. 252.
303. Quoted in Rabbaní, *Priceless Pearl*, p. 40.
304. Letter from Dr Esslemont to Dr Ḥakím, 8 December 1921, in the Archives of the National Spiritual Assembly of the Bahá'ís of the United Kingdom.
305. Quoted in Rabbaní, *Priceless Pearl*, pp. 40–1.
306. Quoted in ibid. pp. 41–2.
307. Letter from Dr Esslemont to Dr Ḥakím, 8 December 1921, in the Archives of the National Spiritual Assembly of the Bahá'ís of the United Kingdom.
308. Florence Pinchon's Memoirs of Dr Esslemont in the Archives of the National Spiritual Assembly of the Bahá'ís of the United Kingdom.
309. Letter from Isobel Slade to the author, 19 May 1969.

310. Letter from E. C. Foster to the author, 10 May 1969.
311. Rabbaní, *Priceless Pearl*, p. 42.
312. 'Abdu'l-Bahá, *Will and Testament*, p. 11.
313. Isaiah 11:6.
314. Quoted in Shoghi Effendi, *God Passes By*, p. 184.
315. Shoghi Effendi, *Promised Day is Come*, p. 124.
316. ibid. p. 17.
317. Shoghi Effendi, *God Passes By*, p. 412.
318. Shoghi Effendi, *Citadel of Faith*, p. 157.
319. ibid. p. 50.
320. ibid. p. 150.
321. Shoghi Effendi, *Messages to the Bahá'í World*, p. 120.
322. ibid. p. 126.
323. Shoghi Effendi, *Messages to the Bahá'í World*, p. 127.
324. Charles Mason Remey.
325. Shoghi Effendi, *Bahá'í Administration*, p. 196.